Liquid Times

Liquid Times

Living in an Age of Uncertainty

ZYGMUNT BAUMAN

polity

First published in 2007 by Polity Press
Reprinted in 2007, 2008

Polity Press
65 Bridge Street
Cambridge CB2 1UR, UK

Polity Press
350 Main Street
Malden, MA 02148, USA

ISBN-10: 0-7456-3986-0
ISBN-13: 978-07456-3986-4
ISBN-10: 0-7456-3987-9 (pb)
ISBN-13: 978-07456-3987-1 (pb)

A catalogue record for this book is available from the British Library.

Typeset in 10.5 on 12 pt Plantin
by Servis Filmsetting Ltd, Manchester
Printed and bound in the United States by Odyssey Press Inc., Gonic, New Hampshire

Every effort has been made to trace all copyright holders, but if any have been inadvertently overlooked the publishers will be pleased to include any necessary credits in any subsequent reprint or edition.

For further information on Polity, visit our website: www.polity.co.uk

Contents

Introduction: Bravely into the Hotbed of
   Uncertainties   1

1 Liquid Modern Life and its Fears   5

2 Humanity on the Move   27

3 State, Democracy and the Management of
   Fears   55

4 Out of Touch Together   71

5 Utopia in the Age of Uncertainty   94

Notes   111

Bravely into the Hotbed
of Uncertainties

At least in the 'developed' part of the planet, a few seminal and closely interconnected departures have happened, or are happening currently, that create a new and indeed unprecedented setting for individual life pursuits, raising a series of challenges never before encountered.

First of all, the passage from the 'solid' to a 'liquid' phase of modernity: that is, into a condition in which social forms (structures that limit individual choices, institutions that guard repetitions of routines, patterns of acceptable behaviour) can no longer (and are not expected) to keep their shape for long, because they decompose and melt faster than the time it takes to cast them, and once they are cast for them to set. Forms, whether already present or only adumbrated, are unlikely to be given enough time to solidify, and cannot serve as frames of reference for human actions and long-term life strategies because of their short life expectation: indeed, a life expectation shorter than the time it takes to develop a cohesive and consistent strategy, and still shorter than the fulfilment of an individual 'life project' requires.

Second, the separation and pending divorce of power and politics, the couple that since the emergence of the modern state and until quite recently was expected to share their joint nation-state household 'till death did them part'.

Much of the power to act effectively that was previously available to the modern state is now moving away to the politically uncontrolled global (and in many ways extraterritorial) space; while politics, the ability to decide the direction and purpose of action, is unable to operate effectively at the planetary level since it remains, as before, local. The absence of political control makes the newly emancipated powers into a source of profound and in principle untameable uncertainty, while the dearth of power makes the extant political institutions, their initiatives and undertakings, less and less relevant to the life problems of the nation-state's citizens and for that reason they draw less and less of their attention. Between them, the two interrelated outcomes of the divorce enforce or encourage state organs to drop, transfer away, or (to use the recently fashionable terms of political jargon) to 'subsidiarize' and 'contract out' a growing volume of the functions they previously performed. Abandoned by the state, those functions become a playground for the notoriously capricious and inherently unpredictable market forces and/or are left to the private initiative and care of individuals.

Third, the gradual yet consistent withdrawal or curtailing of communal, state-endorsed insurance against individual failure and ill fortune deprives collective action of much of its past attraction and saps the social foundations of social solidarity; 'community', as a way of referring to the totality of the population inhabiting the sovereign territory of the state, sounds increasingly hollow. Interhuman bonds, once woven into a security net worthy of a large and continuous investment of time and effort, and worth the sacrifice of immediate individual interests (or what might be seen as being in an individual's interest), become increasingly frail and admitted to be temporary. Individual exposure to the vagaries of commodity-and-labour markets inspires and promotes division, not unity; it puts a premium on competitive attitudes, while degrading collaboration and team work to the rank of temporary stratagems that need to be suspended or terminated the moment their benefits have been used up. 'Society' is increasingly viewed and treated as a 'network' rather than a 'structure' (let alone a solid 'totality'): it is perceived and treated as a matrix of random connections and disconnections and of an essentially infinite volume of possible permutations.

Fourth, the collapse of long-term thinking, planning and acting, and the disappearance or weakening of social structures in which thinking, planning and acting could be inscribed for a long time to come, leads to a splicing of both political history and individual lives into a series of short-term projects and episodes which are in principle infinite, and do not combine into the kinds of sequences to which concepts like 'development', 'maturation', 'career' or 'progress' (all suggesting a preordained order of succession) could be meaningfully applied. A life so fragmented stimulates 'lateral' rather than 'vertical' orientations. Each next step needs to be a response to a different set of opportunities and a different distribution of odds, and so it calls for a different set of skills and a different arrangement of assets. Past successes do not necessarily increase the probability of future victories, let alone guarantee them; while means successfully tested in the past need to be constantly inspected and revised since they may prove useless or downright counterproductive once circumstances change. A swift and thorough *forgetting* of outdated information and fast ageing habits can be more important for the next success than the memorization of past moves and the building of strategies on a foundation laid by previous *learning*.

Fifth, the responsibility for resolving the quandaries generated by vexingly volatile and constantly changing circumstances is shifted onto the shoulders of individuals – who are now expected to be 'free choosers' and to bear in full the consequences of their choices. The risks involved in every choice may be produced by forces which transcend the comprehension and capacity to act of the individual, but it is the individual's lot and duty to pay their price, because there are no authoritatively endorsed recipes which would allow errors to be avoided if they were properly learned and dutifully followed, or which could be blamed in the case of failure. The virtue proclaimed to serve the individual's interests best is not *conformity* to rules (which at any rate are few and far between, and often mutually contradictory) but *flexibility*: a readiness to change tactics and style at short notice, to abandon commitments and loyalties without regret – and to pursue opportunities according to their current availability, rather than following one's own established preferences.

It is time to ask how these departures modify the range of challenges men and women face in their life pursuits and so, obliquely, influence the way they tend to live their lives. This book is an attempt to do just that. To ask, but not to answer, let alone to pretend to provide definite answers, since it is its author's belief that all answers would be peremptory, premature and potentially misleading. After all, the overall effect of the departures listed above is the necessity to act, to plan actions, to calculate the expected gains and losses of the actions and to evaluate their outcomes under conditions of endemic uncertainty. The best the author has tried to do and felt entitled to do has been to explore the causes of that uncertainty – and perhaps lay bare some of the obstacles that bar their comprehension and so also our ability to face up (singly and above all collectively) to the challenge which any attempt to control them would necessarily present.

1

Liquid Modern Life and its Fears

'If you wish peace, care for justice,' averred ancient wisdom; and unlike knowledge, *wisdom* does not age. Absence of justice is barring the road to peace today as it did two millennia ago. This has not changed. What has changed is that 'justice' is now, unlike in ancient times, a planetary issue, measured and assessed by planetary comparisons – and this for two reasons.

First, on a planet criss-crossed by 'information highways', nothing that happens in any part of the planet can actually, or at least potentially, stay in an *intellectual* 'outside'. No *terra nulla*, no blank spots on the mental map, no unknown, let alone unknowable lands and peoples. The human misery of distant places and remote ways of life, as well as the human profligacy of other distant places and remote ways of life, are displayed by electronic images and brought home as vividly and harrowingly, shamingly or humiliatingly, as is the distress or ostentatious prodigality of the human beings close to home during daily strolls through the town's streets. The injustices out of which models of justice are moulded are no longer confined to immediate neighbourhoods and gleaned out of the 'relative deprivation' or 'wage differentials' by comparison with the neighbours next door, or with the mates next in the social ranking.

Second, on a planet open to the free circulation of capital and commodities, whatever happens in one place has a bearing on how people in all other places live, hope or expect to live. Nothing can be credibly assumed to stay in a *material* 'outside'. Nothing is truly, or can remain for long, indifferent to anything else – untouched and untouching. No well-being of one place is innocent of the misery of another. In Milan Kundera's succinct summary, such 'unity of mankind' as has been brought about by globalization means mainly that 'there is nowhere one can escape to'.[1]

As Jacques Attali pointed out in *La Voie humaine*,[2] half of world trade and more than half of global investment benefit just twenty-two countries accommodating a mere 14 per cent of the world's population, whereas the forty-nine poorest countries inhabited by 11 per cent of the world's population receive between them only a 0.5 per cent share of the global product – just about the same as the combined income of the three wealthiest men of the planet. Ninety per cent of the total wealth of the planet remains in the hands of just 1 per cent of the planet's inhabitants. And there are no breakwaters in sight capable of stemming the global tide of income polarization – still ominously rising.

The pressures aimed at the piercing and dismantling of boundaries, commonly called 'globalization', have done their job; with few, and fast disappearing exceptions; all societies lie now fully and truly wide open, materially and intellectually. Add together both kinds of 'openness' – intellectual and material – and you'll see why any injury, relative deprivation or contrived indolence anywhere comes topped up with the insult of injustice: of the feeling of wrong having been done, a wrong crying out to be repaired, but first of all obliging the victims to avenge their ills . . .

The 'openness' of the open society has acquired a new gloss, undreamt of by Karl Popper who coined the term. As before, it means a society frankly admitting its own incompleteness and therefore anxious to attend to its own as yet un-intuited, let alone explored, possibilities; but in addition it means a society impotent, as never before, to decide its own course with any degree of certainty, and to protect the chosen itinerary once it has been selected. Once a precious yet frail product of brave though stressful *self-assertion*, the attribute of 'openness' is mostly associated these days with an irresistible *fate*; with the unplanned and unanticipated side-effects of 'negative globalization' – that is, a selective globalization of trade and capital, surveillance and information, violence and weapons, crime and terrorism, all unanimous in their disdain of the principle of territorial sovereignty and their lack of respect for any state boundary. A society that is 'open' is a society exposed to the blows of 'fate'.

If the idea of an 'open society' originally stood for the self-determination of a free society cherishing its openness, it now brings to most minds the terrifying experience of a heteronomous, hapless and vulnerable population confronted with, and possibly overwhelmed by forces it neither controls nor fully understands; a population horrified by its own undefendability and obsessed with the tightness of its frontiers and the security of the individuals living inside them – while it is precisely that impermeability of its borders and security of life inside those borders that elude its grasp and seem bound to remain elusive as long as the planet is subjected to solely *negative* globalization. On a negatively globalized planet, security cannot be obtained, let alone assured, within just one country or in a selected group of countries: not by their own means alone, and not independently of what happens in the rest of the world.

Neither can justice, that preliminary condition of lasting peace, be so attained, let alone guaranteed. The perverted 'openness' of societies enforced by negative globalization is itself the prime cause of injustice and so, obliquely, of conflict and violence. As Arundhati Roy puts it, 'when the elite, somewhere at the top of the world, pursue their travels to imagined destinations, the poor stay caught in a spiral of crime and chaos.'[3] The actions of the United States government, says Roy, together with its various satellites barely disguised as 'international institutions', like the World Bank, the International Monetary Fund and the World Trade Organization, have brought about, as their 'dangerous side-products', 'nationalism, religious fanaticism, fascism and, of course, terrorism – which advance hand in hand with the progress of liberal globalization'.

'Markets without frontiers' is a recipe for injustice, and for the new world disorder in which the famed formula of Clausewitz has been reversed so that it is the turn of politics to become a continuation of war by other means. Deregulation, resulting in planetary lawlessness, and armed violence feed each other, mutually reinforce and reinvigorate one another; as another ancient wisdom warns, *inter arma silent leges* (when arms speak, laws keep silent).

Before sending troops to Iraq, Donald Rumsfeld declared that the 'war will be won when Americans feel secure again'.[4] That message has been repeated ever since – day in, day out – by George W. Bush. But sending troops to Iraq lifted and continues to lift the fear of insecurity, in the United States and elsewhere, to new heights.

As might have been expected, the feeling of security was not the sole collateral casualty of war. Personal freedoms and democracy soon shared its lot. To quote Alexander Hamilton's prophetic warning,

> The violent destruction of life and property incident to war, the continual effort and alarm attendant on a state of continual danger, will compel nations the most attached to liberty to resort for repose and security to institutions which have a tendency to destroy their civil and political rights. To be

more safe, they at length become willing to run the risk of being less free.[5]

That prophecy is now coming true.

Once visited upon the human world, fear acquires its own momentum and developmental logic and needs little attention and hardly any additional investment to grow and spread – unstoppably. In David L. Altheide's words, it is not fear of danger that is most critical, but rather what this fear can expand into, what it can become.[6] Social life changes when people live behind walls, hire guards, drive armoured vehicles, carry mace and handguns, and take martial arts classes. The problem is that these activities reaffirm and help produce the sense of disorder that our actions are aimed at preventing.

Fears prompt us to take defensive action. When it is taken, defensive action gives immediacy and tangibility to fear. It is our responses that recast the sombre premonitions as daily reality, making the word flesh. Fear has now settled inside, saturating our daily routines; it hardly needs further stimuli from outside, since the actions it prompts day in, day out supply all the motivation and all the energy it needs to reproduce itself. Among the mechanisms vying to approximate to the dream model of *perpetuum mobile*, the self-reproduction of the tangle of fear and fear-inspired actions comes closest to claiming pride of place.

It looks as if our fears have become self-perpetuating and self-reinforcing; as if they have acquired a momentum of their own – and can go on growing by drawing exclusively on their own resources. That ostensible self-sufficiency is of course only an illusion, just as it was in the case of numerous other mechanisms claiming the miracle of self-propelling and self-nourishing perpetual motion. Obviously, the cycle of fear and of actions dictated by fear would not roll on so smoothly and go on gathering speed were it not continuing to draw its energy from existential tremors.

The presence of such tremors is not exactly news; existential quakes have accompanied humans through the whole of their history, because none of the social settings within which human life pursuits have been conducted have ever offered foolproof insurance against the blows of 'fate' (so called in order to set blows of such a kind apart from the adversities human beings *could* avert, and to convey not so much the peculiar nature of these blows as such, as the recognition of humans' *inability to predict them*, let alone to prevent or tame them). By definition, 'fate' strikes without warning and is indifferent to what its victims might do or might abstain from doing in order to escape its blows. 'Fate' stands for human ignorance and helplessness, and owes its awesome, frightening power to those very weaknesses of its victims. And, as the editors of the *Hedgehog Review* wrote in their introduction to the special issue dedicated to fear, 'in the absence of existential comfort' people tend to settle 'for safety, or the pretence of safety'.[7]

The ground on which our life prospects are presumed to rest is admittedly shaky – as are our jobs and the companies that offer them, our partners and networks of friends, the standing we enjoy in wider society and the self-esteem and self-confidence that come with it. 'Progress', once the most extreme manifestation of radical optimism and a promise of universally shared and lasting happiness, has moved all the way to the opposite, dystopian and fatalistic pole of anticipation: it now stands for the threat of a relentless and inescapable change that instead of auguring peace and respite portends nothing but continuous crisis and strain and forbids a moment of rest. Progress has turned into a sort of endless and uninterrupted game of musical chairs in which a moment of inattention results in irreversible defeat and irrevocable exclusion. Instead of great expectations and sweet dreams, 'progress' evokes an insomnia full of nightmares of 'being left behind' – of missing the train, or falling out of the window of a fast accelerating vehicle.

Unable to slow the mind-boggling pace of change, let alone to predict and control its direction, we focus on things we can, or believe we can, or are assured that we can influence: we try to calculate and minimize the risk that we personally, or those nearest and dearest to us at that moment, might fall victim to the uncounted and uncountable dangers which the opaque world and its uncertain future are suspected to hold in store for us. We are engrossed in spying out 'the seven signs of cancer' or 'the five symptoms of depression', or in exorcising the spectre of high blood pressure, a high cholesterol level, stress or obesity. In other words, we seek *substitute* targets on which to unload the surplus existential fear that has been barred from its natural outlets, and we find such makeshift targets in taking elaborate precautions against inhaling someone else's cigarette smoke, ingesting fatty food or 'bad' bacteria (while avidly swilling the liquids which promise to contain the 'good' ones), exposure to sun, or unprotected sex. Those of us who can afford it fortify ourselves against all visible and invisible, present or anticipated, known or as yet unfamiliar, diffuse but ubiquitous dangers through locking ourselves behind walls, stuffing the approaches to our living quarters with TV cameras, hiring armed guards, driving armoured vehicles (like the notorious SUVs), wearing armoured clothing (like 'big-soled shoes') or taking martial arts classes. 'The problem', to quote David L. Altheide once more, 'is that these activities reaffirm and help produce a sense of disorder that our actions precipitate.' Each extra lock on the entry door in response to successive rumours of foreign-looking criminals in cloaks full of daggers and each next revision of the diet in response to a successive 'food panic' makes the world look *more* treacherous and fearsome, and prompts *more* defensive actions – that will, alas, add more vigour to the self-propagating capacity of fear.

A lot of commercial capital can be garnered from insecurity and fear; and it is. 'Advertisers', comments Stephen Graham, 'have been deliberately exploiting widespread fears of catastrophic terrorism, to further increase sales of highly profitable SUVs.'[8] The gas-guzzling military monsters grossly misnamed 'sport utility vehicles' that have already reached 45 per cent of all car sales in the US are being enrolled into urban daily life as 'defensive capsules'. The SUV is

> a signifier of safety that, like the gated communities into which they so often drive, is portrayed in advertisements as being immune to the risky and unpredictable urban life outside . . . Such vehicles seem to assuage the fear that the urban middle classes feel when moving – or queuing in traffic – in their 'homeland' city.

Like liquid cash ready for any kind of investment, the capital of fear can be turned to any kind of profit, commercial or political. And it is. And so it is *personal safety* that has become a major, perhaps even *the* major selling point in all sorts of marketing strategies. 'Law and order', increasingly reduced to the promise of personal (more to the point, *bodily*) safety, has become a major, perhaps *the* major selling point in political manifestos and electoral campaigns; while the display of threats to personal safety has become a major, perhaps *the* major asset in the ratings war of the mass media, constantly replenishing the capital of fear and adding still more to the success of both its marketing and political uses. As Ray Surette puts it, the world as seen on TV resembles 'citizen-sheep' being protected from 'wolves-criminals' by 'sheep dogs – police'.[9]

The most seminal distinction of the present-day avatars of the fears that were otherwise familiar in all previously lived varieties of human existence is perhaps the decoupling of fear-inspired actions from the existential tremors that generate the fear which inspired them. In other words: the displacement of fear – from the cracks and fissures in the human condition where 'fate' is hatched and incubated, to areas of life largely unconnected to the genuine source of anxiety. No amount of effort invested in those areas is likely to neutralize or block the source, and so it proves impotent to placate the anxiety, however earnest and ingenious that effort might be. It is for this reason that the vicious circle of fear and fear-inspired actions rolls on, losing none of its impetus – yet coming no nearer to its ostensible objective.

Let us state explicitly what has been implied before: the vicious circle in question has been displaced/shifted from the area of security (that is, of self-confidence and self-assurance, or their absence) to that of safety (that is, of being sheltered from, or exposed to, threats to one's own person and its extensions).

The first area, progressively stripped of institutionalized, state-endorsed and state-supported protection, has been exposed to the vagaries of the market; it has been turned by the same token into a playground of global forces beyond the reach of political control, and so also beyond the ability of the affected to respond adequately, let alone to effectively resist the blows. Communally endorsed insurance policies against individual misfortunes, which in the course of the last century came to be known collectively under the name of the social ('welfare') state, are now being wholly or partly withdrawn and cut back below the threshold at which their level is capable of validating and sustaining the sentiment of security, and so also the actors' self-confidence. Whatever remains of the extant institutions embodying the original promise moreover no longer offers the hope, let alone the trust, that it will survive further, and imminent, rounds of reductions.

With the state-built and state-serviced defences against existential tremors progressively dismantled, and the arrangements for collective self-defence, such as trade unions and other instruments for collective bargaining, increasingly disempowered by the pressures of market competition that erode the solidarities of the weak – it is now left to individuals to seek, find and practise individual solutions to socially produced troubles, and to try all that through individual, solitary actions, while being equipped with tools and resources that are blatantly inadequate to the task.

The messages addressed from the sites of political power to the resourceful and the hapless alike present 'more flexibility' as the sole cure for an already unbearable insecurity – and so paint the prospect of yet more uncertainty, yet more privatization of troubles, yet more loneliness and impotence, and indeed more uncertainty still. They preclude the possibility of existential security which rests on collective foundations and so offer no inducement to solidary actions; instead, they encourage their listeners to focus on their individual survival in the style of 'everyone for himself, and the devil take the hindmost' – in an incurably fragmented and atomized, and so increasingly uncertain and unpredictable world.

The retreat of the state from the function on which its claims to legitimation were founded for the better part of the past century throws the issue of legitimation wide open again. A new citizenship consensus ('constitutional patriotism', to deploy Jürgen Habermas's term) cannot be presently built in the way it used to be built not so long ago: through the assurance of constitutional protection against the vagaries of the market, notorious for playing havoc with social standings and for sapping rights to social esteem and personal dignity. The integrity of the political body in its currently most common form of a nation-state is in trouble, and so an alternative legitimation is urgently needed and sought.

In the light of what has been discussed before, it is not at all surprising that an alternative legitimation of state authority and another political formula for the benefits of dutiful citizenship are currently being sought in the state's promise to protect its citizens against dangers to *personal safety*. The spectre of social degradation against which the *social* state swore to insure its citizens is being replaced in the political formula of the 'personal safety state' by threats of a paedophile on the loose, of a serial killer, an obtrusive beggar, a mugger, stalker, poisoner, terrorist, or better still by all such threats rolled into one in the figure of an illegal immigrant, against whom the modern state in its most recent avatar promises to defend its subjects.

In October 2004, BBC2 broadcast a documentary series under the title *The Power of Nightmares: The Rise of the Politics of Fear*.[10] Adam Curtis, the writer and producer of the series and one of the most acclaimed makers of serious television programmes in Britain, pointed out that while global terrorism is undoubtedly an all-too-real danger continually reproduced inside the 'no man's land' of the global wilderness, a good deal if not most of its officially estimated threat 'is a fantasy that has been exaggerated and distorted by politicians. It is a dark illusion that has spread unquestioned through governments around the world, the security services, and the international media'. It wouldn't be too difficult to trace the reasons for the rapid and spectacular career of that illusion: 'In an age when all the grand ideas have lost credibility, fear of a phantom enemy is all the politicians have left to maintain their power.'

Numerous signals of the imminent shift in legitimation by state power to that of the personal safety state were there to be spotted well before 11 September, even if people needed, it appears, the shock of the falling towers in Manhattan to be reproduced in slow motion for months on end on millions of TV screens for the news to sink in and be absorbed – and for the politicians to reharness popular existential anxieties to the new political formula. The presidential battle between Jacques Chirac and Lionel Jospin in France took the form of a public auction, with two political leaders vying to outstrip each other in promises of yet greater flexing of muscles in the war against crime, leading to more stringent and severe legislation and ever cleverer and more imaginative punishments for juvenile or grown-up delinquents and the alien and alienating 'strangers in our midst'. When George W. Bush used toughness in the 'war on terror' in his fight to repulse the challenge of his contender, and when the British leader of the opposition attempted to unsettle the 'New Labour' government by focusing the diffuse existential anxieties arising from deregulated labour markets on the threats presented by gypsy travellers and homeless immigrants, the seeds of fear they sowed fell on soil that was already well prepared.

It was not a mere coincidence that (according to Hugues Lagrange)[11] the most spectacular 'safety panics' and the loudest alarms about rising criminality, coupled with ostentatiously tough actions by governments and manifested among other ways in a rapidly rising prison population (the 'substitution of a prison state for the social state', as Lagrange put it), have occurred since the middle '1960s in the countries with the least developed social services (like Spain, Portugal or Greece), and in the countries where social provision was being drastically reduced (like the United States and Great Britain). No research conducted up to the year 2000 has shown a significant correlation between the severity of penal policy and the volume of criminal offences, though most studies have discovered a strong negative correlation between 'the carceral push' on the one side and 'the proportion of social provision independent of the market' and 'the percentage of GDP diverted to such provision' on the other. All in all, the new focus on crime and on dangers threatening the bodily safety of individuals and their property has been shown beyond reasonable doubt to be intimately related to 'the mood of precariousness', and to follow closely the pace of economic deregulation and of the related substitution of individual self-responsibility for social solidarity.

'There are no terrifying new monsters. It's drawing the poison of the fear,' observed Adam Curtis, commenting on the growing preoccupation with bodily safety. Fear is there, saturating daily human existence as deregulation reaches deep into its foundations and the defensive bastions of civil society fall apart. Fear is there – and drawing on its seemingly inexhaustible and eagerly reproduced supplies in order to rebuild depleted political capital is a temptation many a politician finds difficult to resist. And the strategy of capitalizing on fear is also well entrenched, indeed a tradition reaching back into the early years of the neoliberal assault on the social state.

Long before the events of 11 September, surrender to that temptation – complete with the opportunity to draw on its redoubtable benefits – was already well rehearsed and tested. In a study poignantly and aptly named 'The terrorist, friend of state power',[12] Victor Grotowicz analysed the uses to which, in the late 1970s, the government of the German Federal Republic put the terrorist outrages perpetrated by the Red Army Faction. He found that whereas in 1976 only 7 per cent of German citizens considered personal safety to be a paramount political issue, two years later a considerable majority of Germans viewed it as much more important than the fight against unemployment and inflation. During those two years the nation watched on their TV screens the photo-opportunities picturing the exploits of the rapidly swelling police forces and secret services and listened to the ever bolder auction bids of their politicians promising ever tougher measures to be deployed in the all-out war against the terrorists. Grotowicz also found that whereas the liberal spirit of the original emphasis of the German constitution on individual freedoms had been surreptitiously replaced with the state authoritarianism previously so resented – and while Helmut Schmidt publicly thanked the lawyers for abstaining from testing the conformity of the new Bundestag resolutions to constitutional law – the new legislation played mostly into the hands of the terrorists, enhancing their public visibility, and so obliquely their stature, well beyond the limits they could conceivably attain on their own. Indeed, by common conclusion of the researchers, the violent reactions of the forces of law and order added enormously to the terrorists' popularity. One had to suspect that the manifest function of the new stern and ostentatiously merciless policies, declared to be the eradication of the terrorist threat, was in fact playing second fiddle to their latent function – the effort to shift the grounds of state authority from an area it neither could nor intended to control effectively, to another area, where its power and determination to act could be spectacularly demonstrated, and to almost unanimous public applause. The most evident result of the anti-terrorist campaign was a rapid increase in the volume of fear saturating the whole of society. As to the terrorists, the campaign's declared target, it brought them closer to their own target – the sapping of the values sustaining democracy and respect for human rights – than they could otherwise have dreamt of. We may add that the eventual falling apart of the Red Army Faction, with its disappearance from German life, was not brought about by the repressive police actions; it was due to changed social conditions, no longer fertile to the terrorists' *Weltanschauung* and practices.

Exactly the same may be said of the sad story of Northern Irish terrorism, obviously kept alive and growing in support thanks in large measure to the harsh military response of the British; its ultimate collapse could be ascribed to the Irish economic miracle and to a phenomenon similar to 'metal fatigue', rather than to anything which the British Army did or was capable of doing.

Not much has changed since. As the most recent experience shows (according to Michael Meacher's analysis), the endemic ineffectiveness, or even outright counterproductivity, of military action against modern forms of terrorism continues to be the rule: 'Despite the "war on terror", over the past two years . . . al-Qaida seems to have been more effective than in the two years before 9/11.'[13] Adam Curtis, already quoted, goes a step further, suggesting that al-Qaida barely existed at all except as a vague and diffused idea about 'cleansing a corrupt world through religious violence', and started life as an artefact of lawyers' action; it did not even have a name 'until early 2001, when the American government decided to prosecute Bin Laden in his absence and had to use anti-Mafia laws that required the existence of a named criminal organization'.

Given the nature of contemporary terrorism, the very notion of a 'war on terrorism' is, jarringly, a *contradictio in adiecto*. Modern weapons, conceived and developed in an era of territorial invasion and conquest, are singularly unsuited to locating, striking and destroying extraterritorial, endemically elusive and eminently mobile targets, tiny squads or just single persons travelling light, disappearing from the place of assault as rapidly and inconspicuously as they arrived, and leaving behind few if any traces. Given the nature of the modern weapons at the disposal of the military, the responses to such terrorist acts must be as awkward as shaving with an axe – clumsy and fuzzy, spilling over a much wider area than the one affected by the terrorist outrage, and causing more 'collateral casualties', a greater volume of 'collateral damage', and so also more terror, than the terrorists could possibly produce on their own with the weapons at their disposal (the 'war on terrorism', declared after the terrorist assault on the World Trade Center, has already brought about many more 'collateral victims' among the innocent than the outrage to which it was a response). This circumstance is, to be sure, an integral part of the terrorists' design and the principal source of their strength, which much exceeds the power of their numbers and arms.

Unlike their declared enemies, the terrorists need not feel constrained by the limited resources they themselves command. When they work out their strategic designs and tactical plans, they can include among their assets the expected and well-nigh certain reactions of the 'enemy', which are bound to considerably magnify the intended impact of their own atrocity. If the purpose of the terrorists is to spread terror among the enemy population, the enemy army and police will certainly see to it that the purpose is achieved far beyond the degree to which the terrorists themselves would be able to stretch their own capacity.

Indeed, one can only repeat after Meacher: more often than not, and most certainly after 11 September, we seem to be 'playing Bin Laden's game'. This is, as Meacher rightly insists, a lethally flawed policy. I'd add that agreeing to play Bin Laden's game is even less forgivable because, while it is justified in public by the intention to eradicate the terrorist scourge, it seems to follow instead an altogether different logic from the one which such an intention would inspire and justify.

Meacher accuses the governments in charge of the 'war on terrorism' with an

> unwillingness to contemplate what lies behind the hatred: why scores of young people are prepared to blow themselves up, why nineteen highly educated young men were ready to destroy themselves and thousands of others in the 9/11 hijackings, and why resistance [in Iraq] is growing despite the likelihood of insurgents being killed.

Instead of pausing for this sort of contemplation, governments act (and in all probability, some of them, notably the United States, are intending to continue in the same style, as the appointment of John R. Bolton of 'United Nations do not exist' fame as the American representative to the UN has vividly testified). As Maurice Druon has pointed out, 'before launching its war on Iraq, the American government had only four agents [supplying intelligence], who moreover were all double agents.'[14] The Americans started the war assured 'that American troops would be welcome as liberators, with open arms and flowers'. But, to quote Meacher once more, 'the death of more than 10,000 civilians, with 20,000 injured and even higher Iraqi military casualties, is exacerbated, one year on, by the failure to deliver key public services . . . rampant unemployment and a gratuitously heavy-handed US military.' One can only conclude that whereas a thought not followed by action would admittedly be ineffective, thoughtless actions prove to be just as toothless – and this on the top of the enormous increase in the volume of moral corruption and human suffering they were bound to cause.

Terrorist forces will hardly budge under these and similar blows; on the contrary, it is precisely from the clumsiness and the extravagant and wasteful prodigality of their adversary that they draw and replenish their strength. Excess is not only the mark of the explicitly anti-terrorist operations; it is salient as well in the alerts and warnings addressed to their own populations by the anti-terrorist coalition. As Deborah Orr observed more than a year ago, 'many flights are intercepted, yet are never found to have been actually under threat . . . The tanks and troops were stationed outside Heathrow, even though they eventually withdrew without finding anything at all.'[15] Or take the case of the 'ricin factory', whose discovery was publicly and vociferously announced in 2003 and immediately 'trumpeted as "powerful evidence of the continued terrorist threat", although in the end the germ warfare factory at Porton Down couldn't prove that any ricin had ever been in the flat touted as a significant terrorist base'. Indeed, as Duncan Campbell reported from the courts where the alleged 'ricin conspirators' were judged,[16] the only document on which the case was based had already been proved at an early stage to be an 'exact copy of pages on an internet site in Palo Alto, California'; no link to Kabul or al-Qaida could be found; and the prosecution felt obliged to drop the charge. That did not stop the then Home Secretary, David Blunkett, from announcing two weeks later that 'Al Qaida and the international network is seen to be, and will be demonstrated through the courts over the months to come to be, actually on our doorstep and threatening our lives', whereas in the US Colin Powell used the alleged 'London ricin ring' as a proof that 'Iraq and Osama Bin-Laden were supporting and directing terrorist poison cells throughout Europe'. All in all, although 500 people had been held under the new terrorist laws up to the beginning of February 2004, only two were convicted.

Orr points out that as a result of all such inanities the hypothesis of powerful trade interests being instrumental in fanning the terrorist scare must acquire at least some credibility. Ample data may show such a suspicion to be credible. There are indications that the 'war on terror' has considerably increased, instead of combating, the worldwide proliferation of trade in small weapons (the authors of a joint report by Amnesty International and Oxfam estimate that small weapons, 'the real weapons of mass destruction', kill half a million people each year).[17] The profits which American producers and traders of 'self-defense stuff and gadgets' make out of popular fears, which in turn are beefed up and magnified by the very ubiquity and high visibility of such stuff and gadgets, have also been amply documented. All the same, it needs to be repeated that the staple and the most massive product of the war waged against the terrorists accused of sowing fear has thus far been the fear itself.

Another highly visible product of that war has been the far-reaching constraints imposed on personal freedoms – some of them unheard of since the time of the Magna Charta. Conor Gearty, Professor of Human Rights Law at the London School of Economics, lists a long inventory of laws limiting human liberties which have already been passed in Britain under the rubric of 'anti-terrorist legislation',[18] going on to agree with numerous other worried commentators that it is by no means certain whether 'our civil liberties will still be here when we seek to pass them on to our children'. The British judiciary has so far complied with the governmental policy that 'there is no alternative to repression' – and so, as Gearty concludes, 'only liberal idealists' and other similarly gullible well-wishers may 'expect the judicial branch to lead society' in the defence of civil liberties in this 'time of crisis'.

The stories about the sinister exploits inside the Guantanamo camp or Abu-Ghraib prison, cut off not only from visitors but from any national or international law, and about the gradual but relentless descent into inhumanity of men and women appointed to perpetrate or supervise that lawlessness, have been publicized in the press widely enough to save us from repeating them here. What we think of less often, however, and what we seldom hear, is that the demons that surfaced in those remote places may be only some particularly extreme, radical and impudent, wild and reckless specimens of a larger family of lemures that haunt the attics and cellars of our homes right here – in the world where few if any people continue to believe that changing the life of others is of any relevance to their own life. In a world, in other words, in which each individual is left on his or her own while most individuals are tools of each other's promotion.

The solitary life of such individuals may be joyous and is likely to be busy – but it is bound to be risky and fearful as well. In such a world there are not many rocks left on which struggling individuals can build their hopes of rescue and on which they can rely in case of personal failure. Human bonds are comfortably loose, but for that same reason frightfully unreliable, and solidarity is as difficult to practise as its benefits, and even more its moral virtues, are difficult to comprehend.

The new individualism, the fading of human bonds and the wilting of solidarity are engraved on one side of a coin whose other side shows the misty contours of 'negative globalization'. In its present, purely negative form, globalization is a parasitic and predatory process, feeding on the potency sucked out of the bodies of nation-states and their subjects. To quote Attali one more time, the nations organized into states 'lose their influence on the general direction of things and in the process of globalization forfeit all the means they will need to orient their destiny and resist the numerous forms their fears may take'.

Society is no longer protected by the state, or at least it is unlikely to trust the protection on offer; it is now exposed to the rapacity of forces it does not control and no longer hopes or intends to recapture and subdue. It is for that reason, in the first place, that state governments struggling day in, day out to weather the current storms stumble from one ad hoc crisis-management campaign and one set of emergency measures to another, dreaming of nothing more than staying in power after the next election but otherwise devoid of far-sighted programmes or ambitions, not to mention visions of a radical resolution to the nation's recurrent problems. 'Open' and increasingly defenceless on both sides, the nation-state loses its might, now evaporating into global space, and its political acumen and dexterity, now increasingly relegated to the sphere of individual 'life politics' and 'subsidiarized' to individual men and women. Whatever remains of might and politics in the charge of the state and its organs gradually dwindles to a volume perhaps sufficient to furnish not much more than a large-size police precinct. The reduced state can hardly manage to be anything other than a personal safety state.

Having leaked from a society forcefully laid open by the pressures of globalizing forces, power and politics drift ever further in opposite directions. The problem, and the awesome task that will in all probability confront the current century as its paramount challenge, is the bringing of power and politics together again. The reunion of the separated partners inside the domicile of the nation-state is perhaps the least promising of the possible responses to that challenge.

On a negatively globalized planet, all the most fundamental problems – the metaproblems conditioning the tackling of all other problems – are *global*, and being global they admit of no local solutions; there are not, and cannot be, local solutions to globally originated and globally invigorated problems. The reunion of power and politics may be achieved, if at all, at the planetary level. As Benjamin R. Barber poignantly put it, 'no American child may feel safe in its bed if in Karachi or Baghdad children don't feel safe in theirs. Europeans won't boast long of their freedoms if people in other parts of the world remain deprived and humiliated.'[19] No longer can democracy and freedom be fully and truly secure in one country, or even in a group of countries; their defence in a world saturated with injustice and inhabited by billions of humans denied human dignity will inevitably corrupt the very values they are meant to defend. The future of democracy and freedom may be made secure on a planetary scale – or not at all.

Fear is arguably the most sinister of the demons nesting in the open societies of our time. But it is the insecurity of the present and uncertainty about the future that hatch and breed the most awesome and least bearable of our fears. That insecurity and that uncertainty, in their turn, are born of a sense of impotence: we seem to be no longer in control, whether singly, severally or collectively – and to make things still worse we lack the tools that would allow politics to be lifted to the level where power has already settled, so enabling us to recover and repossess control over the forces shaping our shared condition while setting the range of our possibilities and the limits to our freedom to choose: a control which has now slipped or has been torn out of our hands. The demon of fear won't be exorcized until we find (or more precisely *construct*) such tools.

2

Humanity on the Move

A hundred years ago, Rosa Luxemburg suggested that though capitalism 'needs non-capitalist social organizations as the setting for its development' 'it proceeds by assimilating the very condition which alone can ensure its own existence'.[1] Non-capitalist organizations provide a fertile soil for capitalism: capital feeds on the ruins of such organizations, and although this non-capitalist milieu is indispensable for accumulation, the latter proceeds at the cost of this medium nevertheless, by eating it up.

The inborn paradox of capitalism, and in the long run its doom: capitalism is like a snake that feeds on its own tail . . . Alternatively, we may say, using terms unknown to Luxemburg since they were invented only in the last decade or two, a time when the distance between the tail and the stomach was shrinking fast and the difference between the 'eater' and the 'eaten' was becoming ever less visible: capitalism draws its life-giving energy from 'asset stripping', a practice recently brought into the daylight by the common operation of 'hostile mergers', a practice needing ever new assets to be stripped – yet sooner or later, once it is applied globally, supplies are bound to be exhausted, or reduced below the level required for its sustenance. 'Assets' that are 'stripped' are the outcome of other producers' labour – but as those producers are deprived of their assets and so gradually yet relentlessly eliminated, a point is bound to be reached when there are no assets left to be 'stripped'.

In other words, Rosa Luxemburg envisaged a capitalism dying for lack of food: starving to death because it had eaten up the last meadow of 'otherness' on which it grazed. But a hundred years later it seems that a fatal, possibly the *most* fatal result of modernity's global triumph, is the acute crisis of the 'human waste' disposal industry, as each new outpost conquered by capitalist markets adds new thousands or millions to the mass of men and women already deprived of their lands, workshops, and communal safety nets.

Jeremy Seabrook vividly describes the plight of the global poor these days, evicted from their land and forced to seek survival in the fast swelling slums of the nearest megalopolis:

Global poverty is in flight; not because it is chased away by wealth, but because it has been evicted from an exhausted, transformed hinterland . . .

The earth they farmed, addicted to fertiliser and pesticide, no longer yields a surplus to sell in the market. Water is contaminated, irrigation channels are silted up, well water polluted and undrinkable . . . Land was taken by government for a coastal resort, a golf course, or under pressure of structural adjustment plans to export more agricultural products . . . There had been no repairs to school building. The health centre had closed. Forests, where people had always gathered fuel, fruit and bamboo for house repairs, had become forbidden zones, guarded by men in the livery of some private semi-military company.[2]

The volume of humans made redundant by capitalism's global triumph grows unstoppably and comes close now to exceeding the managerial capacity of the planet; there is a plausible prospect of capitalist modernity (or modern capitalism) *choking on its own waste products* which it can neither reassimilate or annihilate, nor detoxify (there are numerous signals of the fast rising toxicity of the rapidly accumulating waste).

Whereas the morbid consequences of industrial and household waste for the ecological balance and for the self-reproducing capacity of life on the planet have been a matter of intense concern for some time now (though far too little action has followed the debates), we have not as yet arrived anywhere near seeing through to and grasping in full the far-reaching effects of the growing masses of *wasted humans* on the political balance and social equilibrium of human planetary coexistence. It is high time, though, to start. In an essentially novel situation like ours neither the examination of the list of usual suspects, nor a resort to the habitual means of tackling them will be of much use in making sense of what is going on – affecting equally, though in a variety of ways, every resident of the planet.

The new 'fullness of the planet' – the global reach of the financial, commodity and labour markets, of capital-managed modernization, and so also of the modern mode of life – has two direct consequences.

The first consequence is the blockage of those outlets that in the past allowed for a regular and timely draining and cleansing of the relatively few modernized and mod-ernizing enclaves of the planet of their 'human surplus', which the modern way of life was bound to produce on an ever rising scale: the superfluous, supernumerary and redundant population – the excess of the rejects of the labour market, and the refuse of the market-targeted economy, over the capacity of recycling arrangements. Once the modern mode of life had spread (or had been forcibly stretched) to encompass the whole of the globe, and so had stopped being the privilege of a limited number of selected countries, the 'empty' or 'no man's' lands (more precisely, lands that thanks to the global power differential could be seen and treated as void and/or masterless by that sector of the planet that was already 'modern'), having served for several centuries as the primary outlet (principal dumping site) for human waste disposal, became thin on the ground and have come close to vanishing altogether. As for the 'redundant humans' who are currently being turned out on a massive scale in the lands that have only recently jumped under (or fallen under) the juggernaut of modernity, such outlets were never available; the need for them did not arise in the so-called 'premodern' societies, innocent of the problem of waste, human or inhuman alike.

In the effect of that double process – of the blocking of the old and the non-provision of new external outlets for human waste disposal – both the 'old moderns' and the newcomers to modernity turn the sharp edge of exclusionary practices increasingly against themselves. Nothing else is to be expected, because the 'difference' that has been encountered/produced in the course of the global expansion of the modern way of life – but could be treated for several centuries as a vexing yet temporary and curable irritant, and handled more or less effectively with the help of 'anthropophagic' or 'anthropoemic' strategies (Claude Lévi-Strauss's terms) – has come home to roost. But at home the customary stratagems tried and tested in faraway lands are not realistic, and all attempts to apply them domestically carry untested, unforeseeable and so terrifying risks.

As Clifford Geertz observed in his trenchant critique of the current choice between the alternatives of the 'application of force to secure conformity to the values of those who possess the force' and 'a vacuous tolerance that, engaging nothing, changes nothing',[3] the power to enforce conformity is no longer available, while 'tolerance' has ceased to be a lofty gesture with which the high and mighty might placate, simultaneously, their own embarrassment and the offence taken by those who felt patronized and insulted by their assumed benevolence. In our times, Geertz points out, 'moral issues stemming from cultural diversity . . . that used to arise . . . mainly between societies . . . now increasingly arise within them. Social and cultural boundaries coincide less and less closely.'

> The day when the American city was the main model of cultural fragmentation and ethnic tumbling is quite gone; the Paris of *nos ancêtres les gaulois* is getting to be about as polyglot, and as polychrome, as Manhattan, and Paris may yet have a North African mayor (or so, anyway, many of the *gaulois* fear) before New York has a Hispanic one . . .
>
> (T)he world is coming at each of its local points to look more like a Kuwaiti bazaar than like an English gentlemen's club . . . *Les milieux* are all *mixtes*. They don't make *Umwelte* like they used to do.

If the excess of population (the part that cannot be reassimilated into 'normal' life patterns and reprocessed back into the category of 'useful' members of society) can be routinely removed and transported beyond the boundaries of the enclosure inside which an economic balance and social equilibrium are sought, people who have escaped transportation and remain inside the enclosure, even if they are momentarily redundant, are earmarked for 'recycling' or 'rehabilitation'. They are 'out' only for the time being, their state of exclusion is an abnormality which commands a cure and musters a therapy; they clearly need to be helped 'back in' as soon as possible. They are the 'reserve army of labour' and must be put into and kept in a decent shape that will allow them to return to active service at the first opportunity.

All that changes, however, once the conduits for draining off the surplus of humans are blocked. The longer the
'redundant' population stays inside and rubs shoulders
with the 'useful' and 'legitimate' rest, the less the lines
separating 'normality' from 'abnormality', temporary inca-
pacitation from final consignment to waste, appear reassuringly unambiguous. Rather than remaining a misery
confined to a relatively small part of the population, as it
used to be perceived, assignment to 'waste' becomes everybody's potential prospect – one of the two poles between
which everybody's present and future social standing oscil-
lates. The habitual tools and stratagems of intervention
that were worked out to deal with an abnormality seen as
temporary and as affecting a minority do not suffice to deal
with the 'problem of waste' in this new form; nor are they
particularly adequate to the task.

Awesome as they may be, all these and similar setbacks
and quandaries tend to be magnified and become yet more
acute in those parts of the globe that have been only recently
confronted with the phenomenon of 'surplus population',
previously unknown to them, and so with the problem of its
disposal. 'Recently' in this case means *belatedly*, at a time
when the planet is already full, when no 'empty lands' are
left to serve as waste disposal sites and when all asymme-
tries of boundaries are turned firmly against newcomers to
the family of moderns. Other lands will not invite other
peoples' surpluses, nor can they, as they themselves were in
the past, be forced to accommodate them. In opposition to
the waste producers of yore, who used to seek and find
global solutions to problems they produced *locally*, those
'latecomers to modernity' are obliged to seek *local* solutions
to *globally* caused problems – with at best meagre, but more
often than not non-existent chances of success.

Whether voluntary or enforced, their surrender to global
pressures, and the consequent opening of their own territory

to the unfettered circulation of capital and commodities, put at risk most of the family and communal businesses which once were able and willing to absorb, employ and support all newly born humans and at most times assured their survival. It is only now that the newcomers to the world of the 'moderns' experience that 'separation of the business from the household', with all its attendant social upheavals and human misery, a process through which the pioneers of modernity went hundreds of years ago and in a form somewhat mitigated by the availability of global solutions to their problems: the abundance of 'empty' and 'no man's lands' that could easily be used to deposit the surplus population that could no longer be absorbed by an economy emancipated from familial and communal constraints. Such a luxury is, emphatically, not available to the latecomers.

Tribal wars and massacres, the proliferation of 'guerrilla armies' or bandit gangs and drug traffickers masquerading as freedom fighters, busy decimating each other's ranks yet absorbing and in due course annihilating the 'population surplus' in the process (mostly the youth, unemployable at home and denied all prospects); this is one of the twisted and perverse 'local quasi-solutions to global problems' to which latecomers to modernity are forced to resort, or rather find themselves resorting. Hundreds of thousands, sometimes millions of people are chased away from their homes, murdered or forced to run for their lives outside the borders of their country. Perhaps the sole thriving industry in the lands of the latecomers (deviously and often deceitfully dubbed 'developing countries') is the *mass production of refugees*.

The ever more prolific products of that industry were what the British prime minister proposed to sweep under other people's carpets by unloading them 'near their home countries', in permanently temporary camps (deviously and often deceitfully dubbed 'safe havens') in order to keep their local problems local – and so as to nip in the bud all attempts of the latecomers to follow the example of the pioneers of modernity by seeking global (and the only effective) solutions to locally manufactured problems. What he proposed in fact (though not in so many words) was to preserve the well-being of his country at the expense of exacerbating the already unmanageable 'surplus population' problems of the immediate neighbours of the latecomers where there is willy-nilly a similar mass production of refugees . . .

Let us note as well that while refusing to share in the effort of 'waste disposal' and 'waste recycling', the affluent West does a lot to invigorate waste *production*; not just indirectly, by dismantling one by one and eliminating as 'unproductive' or 'economically unviable' all past arrangements of anti-waste prophylactics, but directly, through waging globalizing wars and destabilizing ever larger numbers of societies. On the eve of the invasion of Iraq, NATO was asked to mobilize its armies to help Turkey to seal its border with Iraq in view of the impending assault on the country. Many a statesperson of the NATO countries objected, raising many imaginative reservations – but none mentioned publicly that the danger against which Turkey needed (or so it was thought) to be protected was the influx of Iraqi refugees made homeless by the American invasion – not against the invasion of Turkey by an Iraqi army which the American invasion of Iraq was sure to batter and pulverize.[4]

However earnest, the efforts to stem the tide of 'economic migration' are not and probably cannot be made a hundred per cent successful. Protracted misery makes millions desperate, and in an era of the global frontier-land and globalized crime one can hardly expect a shortage of 'businesses' eager to make a buck or a few billion bucks from capitalizing on that desperation. Hence the second formidable consequence of the current great transformation: millions of migrants wandering the routes once trodden by the 'surplus population' discharged by the greenhouses of modernity – only this time in a reverse direction, and unassisted by the armies of *conquistadores*, tradesmen and missionaries. The full dimensions of that consequence and its repercussions are yet to unravel and be grasped in all their many ramifications.

In a brief but sharp exchange of views that took place in 2001 in connection with the war on Afghanistan, Garry Younge mused on the condition of the planet one day *before* 11 September. He recalled 'a boatload of Afghan refugees floating off Australia' (to the applause of 90 per cent of Australians), to be in the end marooned on an uninhabited island in the middle of the Pacific Ocean:

> It is interesting now that they should have been Afghans, given that Australia is very involved in the coalition now, and thinks there is nothing better than a liberated Afghanistan and is prepared to send its bombs to liberate Afghanistan . . . Interesting also that we have now a Foreign Secretary who compares Afghanistan to the Nazis, but who, when he was Home Secretary and a group of Afghans landed at Stansted, said that there was no fear of persecution and sent them back.[5]

Younge concludes that on 10 September the world was 'a lawless place' of which the rich and the poor alike knew that 'might is right', that the high and mighty can ignore and bypass international law (or whatever they choose to call by that name) whenever they find such law inconvenient, and that wealth and power determine not just economics but the morality and politics of the global space, and for that matter everything else concerning the life conditions on the planet.

Somewhat later a case was held before a High Court judge in London to test the legality of the treatment accorded by British authorities to six asylum seekers who were fleeing regimes officially recognized as 'evil', or at least as routinely violating or negligent of human rights – like Iraq, Angola, Rwanda, Ethiopia and Iran.[6] Keir Starmer QC acting on behalf of the six told the judge, Mr Justice Collins, that the new rules introduced in Britain have left hundreds of asylum seekers 'so destitute that they could not pursue their cases'. They slept rough in the streets, were cold, hungry, scared and sick; some were 'reduced to living in telephone boxes and car parks'. They were allowed 'no funds, no accommodation and no food', prohibited to seek paid work while denied access to social benefits. And they had no control whatsoever over when, where (and if) their applications for asylum would be processed. A woman who escaped Rwanda after being repeatedly raped and beaten ended up spending the night on a chair at Croydon police station – allowed to stay on the condition that she would not fall asleep. A man from Angola, who found his father shot and his mother and sister left naked in the street after a multiple rape, ended up denied all support and sleeping rough. In the case presented by Keir Starmer QC, the judge proclaimed the refusal of social assistance unlawful. But the Home Secretary reacted to the verdict angrily: 'Frankly, I am personally fed up with having to deal with a situation where parliament debates issues and the judges then overturn them . . . We don't accept what Mr Justice Collins has said. We will seek to overturn it.'[7] At the same time 200 similar cases were waiting for a court decision.

The plight of the six whose case Keir Starmer QC presented was probably a side-effect of overcrowding and overflowing in the camps, designed or improvised, into which asylum seekers are routinely transported in Britain the moment they land. The numbers of homeless and stateless victims of globalization grow too fast for the planning, location and construction of camps to keep up with them.

One of the most sinister effects of globalization is the deregulation of wars. Most present-day war-like actions, and the most cruel and gory ones among them, are conducted by non-state entities, subject to no state or quasi-state laws and no international conventions. They are simultaneously the outcome, and auxiliary but powerful causes, of the continuous erosion of state sovereignty and continuing frontier-land conditions in 'suprastate' global space. Intertribal antagonisms break out into the open thanks to a weakening of the arms of the state; in the case of the 'new states', of arms that have never been given time (or allowed) to grow muscle. Once let loose, the hostilities render the inchoate or entrenched state-legislated laws unenforceable and for all practical intents and purposes null and void.

The general population of such a state then finds itself in a lawless space; the part of the population that decides to flee the battlefield and manages to escape finds itself in another type of lawlessness, that of the global frontier-land. Once outside the borders of their native country, escapees are in addition deprived of the backing of a recognized state authority that can take them under its protection, vindicate their rights and intercede on their behalf with foreign powers. Refugees are stateless, but stateless in a new sense: their statelessness is raised to an entirely new level by the non-existence or mere ghost-like presence of a state authority to which their statehood could be referred. They are, as Michel Agier put it in his insightful study of refugees in the era of globalization, *hors du nomos* – outside law;[8] not this or that law of this or that country, but *law as such*. They are outcasts and outlaws of a novel kind, the products of globalization and the fullest epitome and incarnation of its frontier-land spirit. To quote Agier again, they have been cast in to a condition of 'liminal drift', and they don't know and cannot know whether it is transitory or permanent. Even if they are stationary for a time, they are on a journey never completed since its destination (whether arrival or return) remains forever unclear, while a place they could call 'final' stays forever inaccessible. They will never be free from a gnawing sense of the transience, indefiniteness and provisional nature of any settlement.

The plight of the Palestinian refugees, many of whom have never experienced life outside the improvised camps hastily patched together more than fifty years ago, has been well documented. As globalization takes its toll, though, new camps (less notorious and largely unnoticed or forgotten) mushroom around the spots of conflagration, prefiguring the model which Tony Blair wished the UN High Commission for Refugees to render obligatory. For instance, the three camps of Dabaab, populated by as many people as the rest of the Kenyan Garissa province in which they were located in 1991–2, show no signs of imminent closure, but more than a decade later they had still failed to appear on a map of the country – still evidently conceived of as temporary features despite their obvious permanence. The same applies to the camps of Ilfo (opened in September 1991), Dagahaley (opened in March 1992) and Hagadera (opened in June 1992).[9]

Once a refugee, forever a refugee. Roads back to the lost (or rather no longer existing) home paradise have been all but cut, and all exits from the purgatory of the camp lead to hell . . . The prospectless succession of empty days inside the perimeter of the camp may be tough to endure, but God forbid that the appointed or voluntary plenipotentiaries of humanity, whose job it is to keep the refugees inside the camp but away from perdition, pull the plug.

And yet they do, time and again, whenever the powers-that-be decide that the exiles are no longer refugees, since ostensibly 'it is safe to return' to that homeland that has long ceased to be their homeland and has nothing that could be offered or that is desired.

There are, for instance, about 900,000 refugees from the intertribal massacres and the battlefields of the uncivil wars waged for decades in Ethiopia and Eritrea, scattered over the northern regions of Sudan (including the ill-famed Darfur), itself an impoverished, war-devastated country, and mingled with other refugees who recall with horror the killing fields of southern Sudan.[10] By a decision of the UN agency endorsed by the non-governmental charities, they are no longer refugees and so are no longer entitled to humanitarian aid. They have refused to go, however; apparently they do not believe that there is 'a home' to which they could 'return', since the homes they remember have been either gutted or stolen. The new task of their humanitarian wardens became therefore to *make* them go . . . In Kassala camp, first the water supplies were cut and then the inmates were forcibly removed beyond the perimeter of the camp, which, just like their homes in Ethiopia, was razed to the ground to bar all thought of return. The same lot was visited on the inmates of Um Gulsam Laffa and Newshagarab camps. According to the testimony of local villagers, about 8,000 inmates perished when the camp hospitals were closed, water wells dismantled and food delivery abandoned. True, it is difficult to verify that story; though what one can be certain of is that hundreds of thousands have already disappeared and continue to disappear from refugee registers and statistics, even if they did not manage to escape from the nowhere-land of non-humanity.

On the way to the camps, their future inmates are stripped of every single element of their identities except one: that of a stateless, placeless, functionless and 'papers-less' refugee. Inside the fences of the camp, they are pulped into a faceless mass, having been denied access to the elementary amenities from which identities are drawn and the usual yarns from which identities are woven. Becoming '*a* refugee' means to lose

> the media on which social existence rests, that is a set of ordinary things and persons that carry meanings – land, house, village, city, parents, possessions, jobs and other daily landmarks. These creatures in drift and waiting have nothing but their 'naked life', whose continuation depends on humanitarian assistance.[11]

As to the latter point, apprehensions abound. Is not the figure of a humanitarian assistant, whether hired or voluntary, itself an important link in the chain of exclusion? There are doubts whether the caring agencies, while doing their best to move people away from danger, do not inadvertently assist the 'ethnic cleansers'. Agier muses on whether the humanitarian worker is not an 'agent of exclusion at a lesser cost', and (more importantly still) a device designed to unload and dissipate the anxiety of the rest of the world, to absolve the guilty and placate the scruples of bystanders, as well as to defuse the sense of urgency and the fear of contingency. Indeed, putting the refugees in the hands of 'humanitarian workers' (and closing one's eyes to the armed guards in the background) seems to be the ideal way to reconcile the irreconcilable: the overwhelming wish to dispose of the noxious human waste while gratifying one's own poignant desire for moral righteousness.

> It may be that the guilty conscience caused by the plight of the damned part of humanity can be healed. To achieve that effect, it will suffice to allow the process of biosegregation, of

conjuring up and fixing identities stained by wars, violence, exodus, diseases, misery and inequality – a process already in full swing – to take its course. The carriers of stigma will be definitely kept at a distance by reason of their lesser humanity, that is their physical as well as moral dehumanization.[12]

Refugees are the very embodiment of 'human waste', with no useful function to play in the land of their arrival and temporary stay, and with neither an intention nor a realistic prospect that they will be assimilated and incorporated into the new social body. From their present dumping site there is no return and no road forward (unless it is a road towards yet more distant places, as in the case of the Afghan refugees escorted by Australian warships to an island far away from all beaten or even unbeaten tracks). A distance large enough to prevent the poisonous effluvia of social decomposition from reaching places inhabited by the natives is the main criterion by which the location of their permanently temporary camps are selected. Out of that place, refugees would be viewed as an obstacle and a trouble; inside that place, they are forgotten. In keeping them there and barring all spilling out, in making the separation final and irreversible, 'the compassion of some and the hatred of others' cooperate in producing the same effect of taking distance and staying at a distance.[13]

Nothing is left but the walls, the barbed wire, the controlled gates, the armed guards. Between them they define the refugees identity – or rather put paid to their right to self-definition, let alone to self-assertion. All waste, including wasted humans, tends to be piled up indiscriminately on the same refuse tip. The act of the assignment to waste puts an end to differences, individualities, idiosyncrasies. Waste has no need of fine distinctions and subtle nuances, unless it is earmarked for recycling; but the refugees'

prospects of being recycled into legitimate and acknowledged members of human society are, to say the least, dim
and infinitely remote. All measures have been taken to
assure the permanence of their exclusion. People without
qualities have been deposited in a territory without denom-
ination, while all roads leading back or forward to mean-
ingful places and to the spots where socially legible
meanings can be and are forged daily have been blocked
for good.

Wherever they go, refugees are unwanted and left in no
doubt that they are. The admittedly 'economic migrants'
(that is people who follow the precept of 'rational choice'
eulogized by the neoliberal chorus, and so try to find a
livelihood where it can be found, rather then staying where
there is none) are openly condemned by the same governments that try hard to make 'flexibility of labour' the prime
virtue of their electorate and that exhort their native unemployed 'to get on their bikes' and go where the buyers of
labour are. But the suspicion of economic motives also
spills over to those newcomers who not so long ago were
seen as exercising their human rights in seeking asylum
from discrimination and persecution. Through repeated
association, the term 'asylum seeker' has acquired a
derogatory flavour. The statesmen of the 'European
Union' deploy most of their time and their brain capacity
in designing ever more sophisticated ways of fortifying
borders and the most expedient procedures for getting rid
of seekers after bread and shelter who have managed to
cross the borders nevertheless.

David Blunkett, as British Home secretary, not to be
outdone, once proposed to blackmail the countries of
origin of refugees into taking back 'disqualified asylum
seekers' by cutting financial aid to those countries that
didn't.[14] This was not his only new idea; Blunkett wished

to 'force the pace of change', complaining that due to the lack of verve among other European leaders 'progress has still been too slow'. He wanted the creation of an all-European 'rapid joint operations force' and 'a taskforce of national experts' to 'draw up common risk assessments identifying weak points in the EU . . . external borders, addressing the issue of seaborne illegal migration and tackling human trafficking' (the new term designed to replace, and defame, the once noble concept of 'passage').

With the active cooperation of governments and other public figures who find in the aiding and abetting of popular prejudices the sole available substitute for facing up to the genuine sources of the existential uncertainty which haunts their electors, 'asylum seekers' have now replaced the evil-eyed witches and other unrepentant evil-doers, the malignant spooks and hobgoblins of former urban legends. The new and rapidly swelling urban folklore puts the victims of the planetary outcasting in the role of the principal 'villains of the piece' – while collecting, collating and recycling the transmitted lore of hair-raising horror stories, for which the insecurities of city life have generated, now and in the past, a constant and ever more avid demand. As Martin Bright has suggested, the infamous anti-immigrant riots in the British town of Wrexham 'were not an isolated event. Attacks on asylum seekers are becoming the norm in the UK.'[15] In Plymouth, for instance, such attacks became routine. 'Sonam, a 23-year-old farmer from Nepal, arrived in Plymouth eight months ago. His cautious smile reveals two missing teeth he lost, not in the violent conflicts in his own country, but coming back from the corner shop in Davenport.'

The hostility of the natives, combined with the authorities' refusal of state benefits to newcomers who fail to claim asylum upon arrival, with funds available for 'humanitarian protection' being trimmed, and with the tough deportation policy aimed at 'unwanted' refugees (10,740 deported in 2002, 1,300 detained pending their deportation in June 2003), have resulted in a sharp drop in asylum applications – from 8,900 in October 2002 to 3,600 in June 2003. The data were triumphantly interpreted by David Blunkett as evidence of the laudable success of the government's policy and clinching proof that 'tough' measures 'were working'. Indeed they were 'working', though the Refugee Council pointed out that 'simply preventing people from entering the UK' can hardly be advertised as a 'success', considering that 'some of these people may be in desperate need of our help'.[16]

Those migrants who, despite the most ingenious of stratagems, could not be expeditiously deported the government proposed to confine to camps possibly to be built in remote and isolated parts of the country (a step transforming the widespread belief that 'the migrants do not want to be or cannot be assimilated into the economic life of the country' into a self-fulfilling prophecy). The government has been busy, as Gary Younge has observed, 'effectively erecting Bantustans around the British countryside, corralling refugees in ways that will leave them isolated and vulnerable'.[17] Asylum seekers, Younge concludes, 'are more likely to be victims of crime than perpetrators'.

Of those on the register of the UNHCR, the UN Refugee Agency, 83.2 per cent are placed in camps in Africa, and 95.9 per cent in Asia. In Europe, so far only 14.3 per cent of the refugees have been locked in camps. But there is little hope so far that the difference in favour of Europe will be upheld for long.

Refugees find themselves in a cross-fire; more exactly, in a double bind.

They are expelled by force or frightened into fleeing their native countries, but refused entry to any other. They do not *change* places; they *lose* their place on earth and are catapulted into a nowhere, into Augé's 'non-lieux' or Garreau's 'nowherevilles', or loaded into Michel Foucault's 'Narrenschiffen', a drifting 'place without a place, that exists by itself, that is closed in on itself and at the same time is given over to the infinity of the sea'[18] – or (as Michel Agier suggests) into a desert, by definition an *un*inhabited land, a land resentful of humans and seldom visited by them.

The camps of refugees or asylum seekers are artifices of temporary installation made permanent through a blocking of their exits. Let me repeat: the inmates of refugee or 'asylum seeker' camps cannot go back 'where they came from', since the countries they left do not want them back, their livelihoods have been destroyed, their homes gutted, razed or stolen – but there is no road forward either, because no government will gladly see an influx of homeless millions, and any government would do its best to prevent the newcomers from settling.

As to their new 'permanently temporary' location, the refugees are 'in it, but not of it'. They do not truly belong to the country on whose territory their cabins have been assembled or their tents pitched. They are separated from the rest of the host country by an invisible, but all the same thick and impenetrable veil of suspicion and resentment. They are suspended in a spatial void where time has ground to a halt. They have neither settled nor are on the move; they are neither sedentary nor nomadic.

In the habitual terms in which human identities are narrated, they are *ineffable*. They are Jacques Derrida's 'undecidables' made flesh. Among people like us, praised by others and priding ourselves on arts of reflection and self-reflection, they are not only un*touch*ables, but un*think*ables. In a world filled to the brim with imagined communities, they are the *unimaginables*. And it is by refusing them the right to be imagined that the others, assembled in genuine or hoping-to-become-genuine communities, seek credibility for their own labours of imagination.

Refugee camps boast a new quality: a 'frozen transience', an ongoing, lasting state of temporaryness, a duration patched together of moments of which none is lived through as an element of, let alone a contribution to, perpetuity. For the inmates of refugee camps, the prospect of long-term sequels and their consequences is not part of the experience. The inmates of refugee camps live, literally, from day to day – and the contents of daily life are unaffected by the knowledge that days combine into months and years. As in the prisons and 'hyperghettoes' scrutinized and vividly described by Loïc Wacquant, encamped refugees 'learn to live, or rather survive [(sur)vivre] from day to day in the immediacy of the moment, bathing in . . . the despair brewing inside the walls'.[19]

Using the terms derived from Loïc Wacquant's analyses,[20] we may say that the refugee camps mix, blend and gel together the distinctive features of both the 'community ghetto' of the Ford–Keynes era and the 'hyperghetto' of our post-Fordist and post-Keynesian times. If 'community ghettos' were relatively self-sustaining and self-reproducing 'mini societies', complete with miniature replicas of the wider society's stratification, functional divisions and the institutions required to serve the complete inventory of communal life's needs, 'hyperghettoes' are anything but self-sustaining communities. They are, we may say, piles of 'cut-off string ends' – artificial and blatantly incomplete collections of the rejected; aggregates, but not communities; topographical condensations unable to survive on their own. Once the elites of the 'community ghettoes' managed to leave and stopped feeding the network of economic ventures that sustained (however precariously) the livelihood of the rest of the ghetto population, the agencies of state-managed care and control (the two functions, as a rule, closely intertwined) moved in. The inmates of the 'hyperghetto' are suspended on strings that originate beyond its boundaries and most certainly beyond its control.

Michel Agier found in the refugee camps some features of 'community ghettoes', but intertwined with the attributes of the 'hyperghetto'.[21] We may surmise that such a combination makes the bond tying the inmates to the camp still stronger. The pull holding together the denizens of the 'community ghetto' and the push condensing the outcasts into a 'hyperghetto', each a powerful force in its own right, here overlap, are superimposed and mutually reinforce each other. In combination with the seething and festering hostility of the outside environment, they jointly generate an overwhelming centripetal force which it is difficult to resist, making all but redundant the infamous techniques of enclosure and isolation developed by the managers and supervisors of Auschwitzes or Gulags. More than any other contrived social microworlds, refugee camps come close to Erving Goffman's ideal type of the 'total institution': they offer, by commission or omission, a 'total life' from which there is no escape, and thereby effectively bar access to any other form of life.

The permanence of transitoriness; the durability of the transient; the objective determination unreflected in the subjective consequentiality of actions; the perpetually underdefined social role, or more correctly an insertion in the life flow without the anchor of a social role; all these and related features of liquid modern life have been exposed and documented in Agier's findings.

One wonders, though, to what extent the refugee camps can be seen as laboratories where (unwittingly perhaps, but no less forcefully for that reason) the new liquid modern 'permanently transient' pattern of life is put to the test and rehearsed . . .

Refugees and immigrants, coming from the 'far away' yet bidding to settle in the neighbourhood, are uniquely suitable for the role of an effigy through which the spectre of 'global forces', feared and resented for doing their job without consulting those whom its outcome is bound to affect, can be burnt. After all, asylum seekers and 'economic migrants' are collective replicas (an alter ego? fellow travellers? mirror images? caricatures?) of the new power elite of the globalized world, widely (and with reason) suspected to be the true villain of the piece. Like that elite, they have no tie to any place, are shifty and unpredictable. Like that elite, they epitomize the unfathomable 'space of flows' where the roots of the present-day precariousness of the human condition are sunk. Seeking other, more adequate outlets in vain, fears and anxieties slide off targets close to hand and re-emerge as popular resentment and fear of the 'aliens nearby'. Uncertainty cannot be defused nor dispersed in a direct confrontation with the other embodiment of extraterritoriality, the global elite drifting beyond the reach of human control. That elite is much too powerful to be confronted and challenged point blank, even if its exact location were known (which it is not). Refugees, on the other hand, hapless and helpless, are a clearly visible, sitting and easy target for unloading the surplus anger, even if they are totally irrelevant to the miseries and fears of more miseries which caused that anger.

Let me add that when faced with an influx of 'outsiders', 'the established' (to deploy Norbert Elias's memorable terms) have every reason to feel threatened. In addition to representing the 'great unknown' which all 'strangers in our midst' embody, these particular outsiders, the refugees, bring home distant noises of war and the stench of gutted homes and scorched villages that cannot but remind the settled how easily the cocoon of their safe and familiar (safe *because* familiar) routine may be pierced or crushed and how deceptive the security of their settlement must be. The refugee, as Bertold Brecht pointed out in *Die Landschaft des Exils*, is 'ein Bote des Unglücks' ('a harbinger of ill tidings').

The 1970s was the decade when the 'glorious thirty years' of postwar reconstruction, social compact and the developmental optimism that accompanied the dismantling of the colonial system and the mushrooming of 'new nations' was falling into the past, opening up the brave new world of erased or punctured boundaries, information deluge, rampant globalization, consumer feasting in the affluent North and a 'deepening sense of desperation and exclusion in a large part of the rest of the world' arising from 'the spectacle of wealth on the one hand and destitution on the other'.[22] We may see it now, with the benefit of hindsight, as a genuine watershed in modern history. By the end of that decade the setting in which men and women faced up to life challenges had been surreptitiously yet radically transformed, invalidating the extant life wisdoms and calling for a thorough revision and overhaul of life strategies.

The blocking of 'global solutions to locally produced problems', and more exactly the present-day crisis of the 'human waste disposal industry', rebounds on the treatment of refugees and asylum seekers by the countries to which the global migrants look in their search for safety from violence, for bread and drinking water; it is also radically changing the plight of the 'internally excluded' inside those countries.

One of the most fateful aspects of change in the treatment accorded to the 'internally excluded' (now renamed 'underclass') was revealed relatively early and has since been thoroughly documented: namely, the passage from a 'social state' model of inclusive community to a 'criminal justice', 'penal', 'crime control' or 'exclusionary' state. David Garland, for instance, observes that

> there has been a marked shift of emphasis from the welfare to the penal modality . . . The penal mode, as well as becoming more prominent, has become more punitive, more expressive, more security-minded . . . The welfare mode, as well as becoming more muted, has become more conditional, more offence-centred, more risk conscious . . .
>
> The offenders . . . are now less likely to be represented in official discourse as socially deprived citizens in need of support. They are depicted instead as culpable, undeserving and somewhat dangerous individuals.[23]

Loïc Wacquant notes a 'redefinition of the state's mission';[24] the state 'retreats from the economic arena, asserting the necessity to reduce its social role to a widening and strengthening of its penal intervention'.

Ulf Hedetoft describes the same aspect of the thirty-year-old transformation from the other (but intimately related) side aimed at the 'externally excluded', the potential immigrants.[25] He notes that 'borders are being redrawn between Us and Them more rigidly' than ever before. Following Andreas and Snyder,[26] Hedetoft suggests that in addition to becoming more selective and diversified in the forms they have assumed, borders have turned into what might be called 'asymmetric membranes': they allow exit, but 'protect against unwanted entrance of units from the other side'. For this purpose, faraway outposts, like controls at other countries' ports of departure by sea and air, have been added to the orthodox immigration checkpoints kept along the territorial frontier line:

stepping up control measures at the external borders, but just as importantly a tighter visa-issuing regime in countries of emigration in 'the South' . . . [Borders] have diversified, as have border controls, taking place not just at the conventional places . . . but in airports, at embassies and consulates, at asylum centres, and in virtual space in the form of stepped-up collaboration between police and immigration authorities in different countries.

As if to supply immediate evidence for Hedetoft's thesis, the British Prime Minister met Ruud Lubbers, the UN High Commissioner for Refugees, to suggest the establishment of 'safe havens' for prospective asylum seekers *near their homes*, that is at a safe distance from Britain and other well-off countries that were until recently their natural destinations. In the typical newspeak of the post-Great Transformation era, the Home Secretary David Blunkett described the topic of the Blair/Lubbers conversation as 'new challenges for developed countries posed by those who used the asylum system as a route to the West' (using that newspeak, one could complain, for instance, of the challenge for the settled people posed by shipwrecked sailors who used the rescue system as a route to dry land).

For the time being, Europe and its overseas outposts (like the United States or Australia) seem to look for an answer to their unfamiliar problems in similarly unfamiliar policies hardly ever practised in European history; policies that are inward rather than outward looking, centripetal rather than centrifugal, implosive rather than explosive – such as retrenchment, falling back upon themselves, building fences topped with a network of X-ray machines and closed circuit television cameras, putting more officials inside the immigration booths and more border guards outside, tightening the nets of immigration and naturalization law, keeping refugees in closely guarded and isolated camps and stopping the others on the approaches to the country well before the migrants reach its borders and had a chance of claiming a refugee or asylum-seeker status – in short, sealing their domain against the crowds knocking on their doors while doing pretty little, if anything at all, to relieve such pressure by removing its causes.

Naomi Klein has noted an ever stronger and more widespread tendency (pioneered by the EU but quickly followed by the US) towards a 'multi-tiered regional stronghold':

> A fortress continent is a bloc of nations that joins forces to extract favourable trade terms from other countries, while patrolling their shared external borders to keep people from those countries out. But if a continent is serious about being a fortress, it also has to invite one or two poor countries within its walls, because somebody has to do the dirty work and heavy lifting.[27]

NAFTA, the US internal market extended to incorporate Canada and Mexico ('after oil,' Naomi Klein points out, 'immigrant labour is the fuel driving the southwest economy' of the US), was supplemented in July 2001 by 'Plan Sur', according to which the Mexican government took responsibility for the massive policing of its southern boundary, effectively stopping the tide of impoverished human waste flowing to the US from Latin American countries. Since then, hundreds of thousands of migrants have been stopped, incarcerated and deported by Mexican police before reaching US borders. As to Fortress Europe, Naomi Klein suggests that 'Poland, Bulgaria, Hungary and the Czech Republic are the postmodern serfs, providing the low-wage factories where clothes, electronics and cars are produced for 20–25 per cent of the cost to make them in Western Europe'. Inside fortress continents, 'a new social hierarchy' has been put in place in an attempt to square the circle, to find a balance between blatantly contradictory yet equally vital postulates: of airtight borders and of easy access to cheap, undemanding, docile labour ready to accept and do whatever is on offer; of free trade and of pandering to anti-immigrant sentiments, that straw at which the governments in charge of the sinking sovereignty of nation-states are clutching to try to salvage their fast crumbling legitimation. 'How do you stay open to business and closed to people?' asks Klein. And answers: 'Easy. First you expand the perimeter. Then you lock down.'

The funds which the European Union transferred most willingly and without haggling to the East and Central European countries even before they were granted membership of the Union were those earmarked for state-of-the-art technology intended to make their eastern borders, shortly to become the eastern borders of 'Fortress Europe', impermeable to outsiders . . .

Perhaps the two trends signalled here are simply two related manifestations of the same enhanced, well-nigh obsessive concerns with security; perhaps they can both be explained by the shift in the balance between the perpetually present inclusivist and exclusionary tendencies; or perhaps they are mutually unrelated phenomena, each subject to its own logic. It can be shown however that whatever their immediate causes, both trends derive from the same root: *the global spread of the modern way of life which by now has reached the furthest limits of the planet*, cancelling the division between 'centre' and 'periphery', or more correctly between 'modern' (or 'developed') and 'premodern' (or 'underdeveloped' or 'backward') forms of life – a division that accompanied the greater part of modern history, when the modern overhaul of received ways was confined to a relatively narrow, though constantly expanding sector of the globe. As long as it remained relatively narrow, that sector could use the resulting power differential as a safety valve to protect itself from overheating, and the rest of the planet as a dumping site for the toxic waste of its own continuous modernization.

The planet, however, is now full; that means, among other things, that typically modern processes like the building of order and economic progress take place everywhere – and so also that 'human waste' is everywhere produced and turned out in an ever rising volume; this time, however, the 'natural' refuse tips suitable for its storage and potential recycling are absent. The process first anticipated by Rosa Luxemburg a century ago (though described by her in mainly economic, rather than explicitly social terms) has reached its ultimate limit.

3

State, Democracy and the Management of Fears

It has been mostly in Europe and its former dominions, overseas offshoots, branches and sedimentations (as well as in a few other 'developed countries' with a European connection of a *Wahlverwandschaft* rather than *Verwandschaft* kind) that the ambient fears and securitarian obsessions have made the most spectacular career in recent years.

When looked at in separation from other seminal departures occurring in those 'recent years', this appears to be a mystery. After all, as Robert Castel rightly points out in his incisive analysis of the current insecurity-fed anxieties, 'we – at least in the developed countries – live undoubtedly in some of the most secure (*sûres*) societies that ever existed.'[1] And yet, contrary to the 'objective evidence', it is precisely the cosseted and pampered 'we' of all people who feel more threatened, insecure and frightened, more inclined to panic, and more passionate about everything related to security and safety than people of most other societies on record.

Sigmund Freud confronted the puzzle of apparently unwarranted fears point blank and suggested that its solution should be sought in the human psyche's staunch defiance of the dry 'logic of facts'.[2] Human suffering (and so also the fear of suffering, that most vexatious and arguably the most aggravating specimen of suffering) arises from the 'superior power of nature, the feebleness of our own bodies and the inadequacy of the regulations which adjust the mutual relationships of human beings in the family, the state and society'.

As to the first two causes named by Freud, we manage one way or another to reconcile ourselves to the ultimate limits of what we can do: we know that we shall never master nature fully and that we won't make our mortal bodies immortal or immune to the merciless flow of time – and so, at least in this area, we are ready to settle for 'second best'. The knowledge of limits, however, may be as stimulating and energizing as it is depressing and disabling: if we cannot remove *all* suffering, we can remove *some* and mitigate *some other* – the matter is worth trying, and trying over and over again. So we do try as much as we can, and our successive trials consume most of our energy and attention, leaving little room for mournful reflection and for the worry that some otherwise desirable improvements will stay definitely out of bounds, making all attempts to reach them a waste of precious time.

It is quite different, however, in case of the third kind of suffering: misery with a genuinely or putatively *social* origin. *Whatever* is made by humans can be remade *by humans*. In this case, therefore, we do not accept any limit to the remaking of reality; we reject the possibility that any limits can be pre-set and fixed once and for all on our undertakings so that they could not be broken with due determination and good will: 'we cannot see why the regulations made by ourselves should not . . . be a protection and a benefit for every one of us.' Any case of socially determined unhappiness is therefore a challenge, a matter of abuse and a call to arms. If the 'really available protection' and the benefits we enjoy stop short of the ideal, if the relationships are still not to our liking, if regulations are not what they should (and as we believe, could) be, we are inclined to suspect at least a reprehensible scarcity of good will, but more often than not we assume some hostile machinations, plots, conspiracy, a criminal intent, an enemy at the gate or under the bed, a culprit with a name and an address yet to be revealed, still to be brought to justice. Malice aforethought, in short.

Castel arrives at a similar conclusion, after finding that modern insecurity does not derive from a *dearth* of protection but from the *'unclarity* of its scope' (*ombre portée*) in a social universe that 'has been organized around an endless pursuit of protection and a frantic search for security'.[3] The poignant and incurable experience of insecurity is a side-effect of the conviction that, given the right skills and proper effort, *full security can be achieved* ('it can be done', 'we can do it'). And so, if it transpires that it has *not* been done, the failure can only be explained by a wicked deed with an evil intention. Of this piece, there must be a villain.

We can say that the modern variety of insecurity is distinctively marked by a fear of *human* maleficence and malefactors. It is shot through by suspicion towards other humans and their intentions and by a refusal to trust the constancy and reliability of human companionship, and it derives in the last account from our inability and/or our unwillingness to make that companionship durable and reliable, and thus trustworthy.

Castel charges modern individualization with the responsibility for such a state of affairs; he suggests that modern society, having replaced the closely knit communities and corporations which once defined the rules of protection and monitored their application with the individual duty of self-interest, self-care and self-help, has been living on the quicksand of contingency. In such a society, the sentiments of existential insecurity and scattered fears of diffuse dangers are, inevitably, endemic.

As in most other modern transformations, Europe played the pioneering role here. Europe was also the first to confront the phenomenon of unanticipated, and as a rule unwholesome consequences of change. The unnerving sense of insecurity would not have sprouted if it had not been for the simultaneous occurrence of two departures taking place in Europe – spreading only later, and with varying speed, to other parts of the planet. The first was, to follow Castel's terminology, the 'over-evaluation' (*survalorisation*)[4] of the individuals liberated from the constraints imposed by the dense network of social bonds. But a second departure followed closely after: an unprecedented frailty and vulnerability of those individuals, stripped of the protection which had been matter-of-factly offered in the past by that dense network of social bonds.

In the first departure, individual human beings saw excitingly and seductively vast expanses unfolded in front of them, where the newly discovered arts of self-constitution and self-improvement could be experimented with and practised. But the second departure barred most individuals from entry into that attractive territory. Being an individual *de jure* (by decree of law or by the salt of personal guilt being rubbed into the wound left by socially induced impotence) by no means guaranteed individuality *de facto*, and many lacked the resources to deploy the rights implied by the first in the struggle for the second.[5] *Fear of inadequacy* is the name of the resulting affliction. For many individuals-by-decree, if not for all, inadequacy was stark reality, not a sombre premonition – but the *fear* of inadequacy became a universal, or near-universal ailment. Whether the genuine reality of inadequacy had been already experienced, or so far had luckily been kept at arm's length, the *spectre* of inadequacy was to haunt the whole of society and all the time.

From the start, the modern state was therefore confronted with the daunting task of the *management of fear*. It had to weave a network of protection from scratch to replace the old one torn apart by the modern revolution, and to go on repairing it as the continuous modernization promoted by that state kept stretching it beyond its capacity and making it fray. Contrary to widespread opinion, it was *protection* (collective insurance against individual ill-fortune) rather than the *redistribution of wealth* that lay at the heart of the 'social state' to which the development of the modern state unyieldingly led. For people deprived of economic, cultural or social capital (all assets, in fact, except their labouring ability, which each could not deploy on his or her own) 'protection can be collective or none at all'.[6]

Unlike the protective social webs of the premodern past, the state-conceived and state-administered networks were either constructed deliberately and by design, or evolved by their own momentum out of the other large-scale construction endeavours characteristic of modernity in its 'solid' phase. Welfare institutions and provision (sometimes called 'social wages'), state-run or state-assisted health services, schooling and housing, as well as the factory laws that spelt out the mutual rights and obligations of all sides in labour buying and selling contracts, and by the same token protected the well-being and entitlements of employees, provide examples of the first category. The foremost instance of the second category was the factory-floor, trade-union and occupational solidarity that took root and flourished 'naturally' in the relatively stable environment of the 'Fordist factory', the epitome of the solid modern setting in which most of those 'lacking other capital' were fixed.

Engagement with the opposite side in capital–labour relations was mutual and long term in the 'Fordist' factory, making both sides dependent on each other – but at the same time enabling them to think and plan for the future, bind the future and invest in the future. The 'Fordist factory' was for that reason a site of bitter conflict, occasionally exploding into open hostility (as the prospect of engagement in the long term and the mutual dependency of all sides made a head-on confrontation a reasonable investment and a sacrifice which would pay off), but at all times it simmered and festered even if it was hidden from view. And yet the same kind of factory was also a secure shelter for trust into the future and so for negotiation, compromise and a search for a consensual mode of cohabitation. With its clearly defined career tracks, tiresome but reassuringly stable routines, slow pace of change in the composition of labour teams, long usefulness of skills once acquired, meaning a high value attached to accumulated work experience, the hazards of the labour market could be held at arm's length, uncertainty could be subdued if not entirely eliminated, and fears could be excised to the marginal realm of 'blows of fate' and 'fatal accidents', instead of saturating the run of daily life. Above all, those many who lacked all capital except their ability to work for others could count on the collectivity. Solidarity reforged their labouring ability into a substitute capital – and a kind of capital that was hoped, not without reason, to counterbalance the combined power of all other capital.

Famously and memorably, T. H. Marshall attempted, shortly after the postwar British 'welfare state' had been established through comprehensive parliamentary legislation, to reconstruct the logic which guided the gradual unravelling of the meaning of individual rights. According to his account,[7] the long process started from the dream of personal security, followed by a long struggle against the arbitrary rule of kings and princes. What for the kings and princes was the divine right to proclaim and disclaim the rules at will, and so in the ultimate account to follow their own whims and caprices, meant for their subjects a life lived at the mercy of a royal benevolence not much different from erratic fate: a life of continuous and incurable uncertainty, depending on the mysterious ways in which sovereign's favours moved. The king's or queen's grace was difficult to curry and yet more difficult to retain; it was easily withdrawn and impossible to secure forever. Such uncertainty rebounded as a humiliating sense of people's own impotence, which couldn't be repaired until the conduct of royal sovereigns was made predictable through being subjected to legal rules which the sovereigns themselves were not allowed and/or were unable to alter or suspend of their own volition, without the consent of the subjects concerned. In other words, personal security could be attained only through the introduction of rules binding *all* players of the game. The universality of rules would not make everybody a winner; as before, there would be lucky and unlucky players, winners and losers. But at least the rules of the game would be made explicit and possible to learn and they would not be changed at whim while the game was still being played; and the winners would not have to fear the king's jaundiced eye, because the fruits of their victory would indeed be theirs to enjoy forever: they would become their inalienable property.

We can say that the fight for personal rights was animated by the desire of those who were already lucky or hoping to win next time to keep the gifts of their good fortune without the need for a costly, cumbersome, and worst of all unreliable and forever inconclusive effort to ingratiate themselves into the sovereign's grace and retain the sovereign's favours.

The demand for *political* rights, that is for playing a substantive part in the making of laws, was according to Marshall next on the agenda, as the logical step to take once *personal* rights had been gained and needed to be defended; yet one can conclude from what has just been said that the two sets of rights, personal and political, could be fought for, attained and made secure only *together* – they could hardly be achieved and enjoyed separately. There seems to be a circular dependency, a veritable 'chicken and egg' relation between the two. The safety of persons and the security of their possessions are indispensable conditions of their ability to fight effectively for the right of political participation, but they can't be firmly grounded and be confidently assumed to last unless the shape of the binding laws has been made dependent on their beneficiaries.

One can't be sure of one's personal rights unless one is able to exercise political rights and make that ability count in the lawmaking process; and the prospects for making that ability count will be dim to say the least unless the assets (economic and social) personally commanded and protected by personal rights are large enough to be reckoned with in the calculations of the powers that be. As was already obvious to T. H. Marshall, but needed to be, in the light of the latest political trends, emphatically restated by Paolo Flores d'Arcais, 'poverty (old and new) generates desperation and subjection, drains all energy in the struggle to survive, and puts the will at the mercy of empty promise and insidious deceit.'[8] The intertwining and interplay of personal and political rights are for the high and mighty – for the rich, not for the poor, for the '*already secure* if only left alone', but not for the 'needing external assistance to *become secure*'. The right to vote (and so, obliquely and at least in theory, the right to influence the composition of the rulers and the shape of the rules that bind the ruled) could be meaningfully exercised only by those 'who possess sufficient economic and cultural resources' to be 'safe from the voluntary or involuntary servitude that cuts off any possible autonomy of choice (and/or its delegation) at the root'.

No wonder that for a long time the promoters of the electoral solution to the quandary of securing personal rights by the exercise of political ones 'wanted to limit suffrage according to wealth and education'. It seemed obvious at the time that 'full freedom' (that is, the right to partake in the lawmaking process) could only be enjoyed by those who possessed the full 'property of their persons'[9] – that is those people whose personal freedom was not truncated by lords of the manor or by employers on whom they depended for their livelihood. For more than a century after the invention and the enthusiastic or resigned acceptance of the project of political representation, the extension of suffrage to anyone except the 'haves' was resisted tooth and nail by the promoters and advocates of their project. Not without reason, the prospect of such an extension was viewed as an assault against democracy rather than its triumph (the tacit assumption adding vigour to that resistance probably being the premonition that the 'have nots' would not use the gift of political participation for the defence of the security of possessions and social standing – the kinds of personal rights in which they themselves had no stake).

To follow Marshall's logical/historical sequence of rights, we may say that up to (and including) the stage of political rights, democracy is a selective and strictly limited adventure; that the *demos* (people) of 'democracy' meant to hold the *kratos* (power) over the creation and alteration of laws is confined at that stage to a privileged few, while excluding, not only in practice but also in the letter of law, a large majority of people whom the politically shaped laws of the country were intended to bind.

Indeed, as John R. Searle has recently reminded us, the inventory of 'God given', that is inalienable rights composed by the Founding Fathers of American democracy 'did not include equal rights for women – not even the right to vote or to own property – and did not include abolition of slavery'.[10] And Searle does not consider that quality of democracy (the quality, we may say, of being a privilege meant to be awarded cautiously and sparingly) to be temporary, transient and now left behind. For instance, 'there will always be views that a lot of people, indeed a majority, find revolting', and so the odds are against a full and truly universal granting of the freedom of speech which political rights are intended to assure to all citizens. But a yet more basic qualification should be added: if political rights can be used to entrench and solidify personal freedoms grounded in economic power, they will hardly assure personal freedoms to the *dispossessed*, who have no claim on the resources without which personal freedom can neither be won nor in practice enjoyed.

One finds here a vicious circle of sorts: a large number of people have only a few if any possessions or acquisitions worthy of a gallant defence, and so in the view of the haves they neither need nor should be entrusted with the political rights expected to serve that purpose. Since however such people are for that reason not admitted to the selected company of electorate (and throughout the history of modern democracy potent forces have fought to make that refusal of admission permanent), they will have little chance to secure the material and cultural resources that would make them eligible for the award of political rights. Left to its own developmental logic, 'democracy' might remain not just in practice, but also formally and explicitly, an essentially elitist affair. But, as Paolo Flores d'Arcais justly observes, there were two, not one, possible solutions to such a quandary: 'either by in fact limiting suffrage to those who already possessed such resources, or by progressively "revolutionizing" society in such a way as to turn those privileges – affluence and culture – into rights guaranteed for all'.

It was the second solution that inspired Lord Beveridge's blueprint for the welfare state, the most comprehensive embodiment of T. H. Marshall's idea of *social* rights – that third in the chain of rights without which the democratic project is bound to stop short of its conclusion. 'A vigorous welfare programme', as d'Arcais sums up his argument more than half a century after Beveridge, 'ought to be an integral, and *constitutionally* protected, part of every democratic project.' Without political rights, people cannot be confident of their personal rights; but without *social* rights, *political* rights will remain an unattainable dream, a useless fiction or a cruel joke for the large number of those to whom they have been granted by the letter of law. If social rights are not assured, the poor and indolent cannot practise the political rights they formally possess. And then the poor will have only such entitlements as governments think it necessary to concede, and as is acceptable to those with the genuine political muscle to gain and keep power. As long as they remain resourceless, the poor may hope at most to be receivers of transfers, not subjects of rights.

Lord Beveridge was right to believe that his vision of comprehensive, collectively endorsed insurance for everyone was the inevitable consequence of the liberal idea as well as an indispensable condition of a fully fledged liberal democracy. Franklin Delano Roosevelt's declaration of war on fear was based on a similar assumption.

Freedom of choice comes together with uncounted and uncountable risks of failure; many people may consider such risks unbearable, finding out or suspecting that they may exceed their personal ability to cope. For most people, freedom of choice will remain an elusive phantom and an idle dream, unless the fear of defeat is mitigated by an insurance policy issued in the name of the community, a policy they can trust and rely on in case of misfortune. As long as it remains a phantom, the pain of hopelessness will be topped by the humiliation of haplessness; the ability to cope with life challenges, tested daily, is after all that very workshop in which confidence in oneself is cast or melted.

Without collectively endorsed insurance, the poor and indolent (and more generally the weak balancing at the verge of exclusion) have no stimulus for political engagement – and certainly not for participation in a democratic game of elections. No salvation is likely to arrive from a political state that is not, and refuses to become, a social state as well. Without social rights for all, a large number of people – and a number likely to grow – will find their political rights useless and unworthy of their attention. If political rights are necessary to set social rights in place, *social* rights are indispensable to keep *political* rights in operation. The two rights need each other for their survival; that survival can only be their *joint* achievement.

The historical records show that with every extension of suffrage societies have moved a step further towards a comprehensive – 'complete' – social state, though that final destination was not visualized in advance and needed many years and several hotly contested yet ever more ambitious parliamentary laws for its contours to become visible. As more categories of population were granted electoral rights, the 'median voter' on whose satisfaction political parties had to orient themselves in order to win, moved steadily to the relatively more deprived parts of the social spectrum. At some point, inevitably though rather unexpectedly, a seminal shift occurred; the line was crossed dividing those who sought political rights in order to make sure that the personal rights they *already enjoyed* would be neither withdrawn nor tinkered with, from those who needed political rights in order to *gain* personal rights they did not yet possess, and who, if granted *personal* (or for that matter *political*) rights unaccompanied by *social* rights, would have found them inoperable.

At that point, the stakes of the political game underwent a genuinely watershed-like change. From the task of *adjusting* the political institutions and procedures to the already existing social realities, modern democracy moved to the task of deploying political institutions and procedures in *reforming* social realities. It moved, in other words, from the task of *conserving* the balance of social forces to that of *changing* it. Paradoxically, it faced the task of reversing the sequence followed thus far: the effect of crossing the threshold was an unfamiliar and hitherto unconfronted task of using political rights to *create* and assure personal rights instead of merely *confirming* them and firming them up. Instead of growing out of an already formed 'civil society' yearning for a political shield, the body politic in its new form of a 'social state' faced the task of laying the foundations of civil society or extending them to accommodate the parts of society where it had thus far been missing.

The specifically modern fears were born during the first bout of deregulation-cum-individualization, at the moment when interhuman kinship and neighbourly bonds, tightly tied by community or corporation knots, apparently eternal but at any rate surviving since time immemorial, had been loosened or broken. The solid modern mode of fear management tended to replace the irreparably damaged 'natural' bonds by their artificial equivalents in the form of associations, unions and part-time yet quasi-permanent collectivities unified by shared interests and daily routines; *solidarity* was to take over from *belonging* as the main shield against increasingly hazardous fate.

The dissipation of solidarity spelled an end to that solid modern fashion of fear management. The turn has now come of the modern, artificial, administered protections to be loosened, dismantled or otherwise broken. Europe, the first to undergo the modern overhaul and the first to run the whole spectrum of its sequels, is now going, much like the United States, through 'deregulation-cum-individualization mark two' – though this time it does not do it of its own choice, but succumbing to the pressure of global forces it can no longer control or hope to check.

This second deregulation has not been followed, however, by new societal forms of fear management; the task of coping with fears emanating from new uncertainties has been, like the fears themselves, deregularized and 'subsidiarized', that is left to local initiatives and efforts, and in large part privatized – transferred in large measure to the sphere of 'life politics', that is left by and large to the care, ingenuity and cunning of individuals, and to the markets, stoutly resenting and effectively resisting all forms of communal (political) interference, let alone control.

Once competition replaces solidarity, individuals find themselves abandoned to their own – pitifully meagre and evidently inadequate – resources. The dilapidation and decomposition of collective bonds made them, without asking their consent, individuals *de jure*, though what they learn from their life pursuits is that virtually everything in the present-day state of affairs militates against their rise to the postulated model of individuals *de facto*. A yawning (and from what we can see widening) gap separates the quantity and the quality of the resources which would be required by an effective production of a do-it-yourself but nonetheless reliable and trustworthy security and genuine freedom from fear, from the sum total of materials, tools and skills which the majority of individuals can reasonably hope to acquire and retain.

Robert Castel signals the return of *dangerous classes*.[11] Let us observe, though, that the similarity between their first and the second coming is partial at best.

The original 'dangerous classes' were made up of the temporarily excluded and not as yet reintegrated population surplus which accelerating economic progress had deprived of a 'useful function', while the accelerating pulverization of networks of bonds had stripped them of protection; but it was hoped that in due course they would be reintegrated again, their resentment dissipated and their stakes in the 'social order' restored. The new 'dangerous classes', on the other hand, are those recognized as *unfit* for reintegration and proclaimed to be unassimilable, since no useful function can be conceived for them to perform after 'rehabilitation'. They are not just excessive, but *redundant*. They are excluded *permanently* – one of the few cases of 'permanence' which liquid modernity not only allows, but actively promotes. Rather than being perceived as the outcome of momentary and repairable bad luck, today's exclusion exudes an air of finality. Ever more often, exclusion tends today to be a one-way street (and to be perceived as such). Once burnt, bridges are unlikely ever to be rebuilt. It is the *irrevocability* of their eviction and the dimness of the chances to appeal against the verdict that makes the contemporary excluded into 'dangerous classes'.

The irrevocability of exclusion is a direct, though unforeseen consequence of the decomposition of the social state – as a web of established institutions, but perhaps even more significantly as an ideal and a project by which realities are judged and actions spurred. The degradation of the ideal and the emaciation and decline of the project portend after all the disappearance of redemptive opportunities and the withdrawal of the right of appeal, and so also a gradual dissipation of hope and a wilting of the will to resist. Rather than being a condition of being '*un*-employed' (the term implying a departure from the norm which is 'to be *employed*', a temporary affliction that can and shall be cured), being out of a job feels increasingly like a state of 'redundancy' – being rejected, branded as superfluous, useless, unemployable and doomed to remain 'economically *in*active'. Being out of a job implies being disposable, perhaps even disposed of already and once and for all, assigned to the waste of 'economic progress' – that change which boils down in the last account to doing the same work and achieving the same economic results but with a smaller workforce and lower 'labour costs' than before.

Only a thin line today separates the unemployed, and especially the long-term unemployed, from a fall into the black hole of the 'underclass': men and women fitting into no legitimate social division, individuals left outside classes and carrying none of the recognized, approved, useful and indispensable functions that 'normal' members of society perform; people who add nothing to the life of society except what society could well do without and would gain from getting rid of.

No less tenuous is the line separating the 'redundant' from criminals: the 'underclass' and 'criminals' are but two subcategories of the excluded, the 'socially unfit' or even 'anti-social elements', differing from each other more by the official classification and the treatment they receive than by their own stance and conduct. Just like the people out of a job, the criminals (that is, those consigned to imprisonment, charged and awaiting trial, under police supervision, or simply on police registers) are no longer viewed as temporarily evicted from normal social life and bound to be 're-educated', 'rehabilitated' and 'returned to the community' at the nearest opportunity – but as permanently marginalized, unfit for 'social recycling' and bound to be kept for the duration out of mischief, and away from the community of the law-abiding.

4

Out of Touch Together

Inhabited areas are described as 'urban' and called 'cities' if they are marked by a relatively high density of population, interaction and communication. Today, they also happen to be the places where socially conceived and incubated insecurities are confronted in a highly condensed and so particularly tangible form. It is also in the places called 'urban' that the high density of human interaction has coincided with the tendency of fear born of insecurity to seek and find outlets and objects on which to unload itself – though this tendency has not always been the distinctive characteristic of these places.

As Nan Ellin, one of the most acute researchers and insightful analysts of contemporary urban trends, points out, protection from danger was 'a principal incentive for building cities whose borders were often defined by vast walls or fences, from the ancient villages of Mesopotamia to medieval cities to Native American settlements'.[1] The walls, moats and stockades marked the boundary between 'us' and 'them', order and wilderness, peace and warfare: enemies were those left on the other side of the fence and not allowed to cross it. 'From being a relatively safe place', however, the city has become associated, mostly in the last hundred years or so, 'more with danger than with safety'.

Today, in a curious reversal of their historical role and in defiance of the original intentions of city builders and the expectations of city dwellers, our cities are swiftly turning from shelters against danger into danger's principal source. Diken and Laustsen go so far as to suggest that the millennia-old 'link between civilization and barbarism is reversed. City life turns into a state of nature characterised by the rule of terror, accompanied by omnipresent fear.'[2]

We can say that the sources of danger have now moved almost wholly into urban areas and settled there. Friends – but also enemies, and above all the elusive and mysterious *strangers* who veer threateningly between the two extremes – now mix and rub shoulders on the city streets. The war against insecurity, and particularly against dangers and risks to personal safety, is now waged *inside* the city, and inside the city battlefields are set aside and front lines are drawn. Heavily armed trenches (impassable approaches) and bunkers (fortified and closely guarded buildings or complexes) aimed at separating, keeping away and barring the entry of strangers, are fast becoming one of the most visible aspects of contemporary cities – though they take many forms, and though their designers try hard to blend their creations into the cityscape, thereby 'normalizing' the state of emergency in which urban residents, addicted to safety yet perpetually unsure of it, dwell daily.

'The more we detach from our immediate surroundings, the more we rely on surveillance of that environment . . . Homes in many urban areas around the world now exist to protect their inhabitants, not to integrate people with their communities,' observe Gumpert and Drucker.[3] Separation and keeping a distance becomes the most common strategy these days in the urban struggle for survival. The continuum along which the results of the struggle are plotted stretches between the poles of voluntary and involuntary urban ghettoes. Residents without means, and for that reason viewed by the rest of the residents as potential threats to their safety, tend to be forced away from the more benign and agreeable parts of the city and crowded in to separate, ghetto-like districts. Resourceful residents buy into separate areas of their choice, also ghetto-like, and bar all others from settling there; in addition, they do whatever they can to disconnect their own lifeworld from the lifeworlds of the rest of the city's inhabitants. Increasingly their voluntary ghettoes turn into the outposts or garrisons of extraterritoriality.

'As their residents extend their communication spaces to the international sphere, they often simultaneously turn their homes away from public life through increasingly "smart" security infrastructures', comment Graham and Marvin.[4]

> Virtually all cities across the world are starting to display spaces and zones that are powerfully connected to other 'valued' spaces across the urban landscape as well as across national, international and even global distances. At the same time, though, there is often a palpable and increasing sense of local disconnection in such places from physically close, but socially and economically distant, places and people.[5]

The waste products of the new physical extraterritoriality of the privileged urban spaces inhabited and used by the global elite – the elite's 'internal exile' of sorts achieved through, manifested in and sustained by means of 'virtual connectedness' – are the disconnected and abandoned spaces; the 'ghost wards', as they have been called by Michael Schwarzer, places where 'dreams have been replaced by nightmares and danger and violence are more commonplace than elsewhere'.[6] If distances are intended to be kept impassable so as to stave off the danger of leakage and the contamination of regional purity, a policy

of zero tolerance comes in handy, together with the ban-
ishment of the homeless from the spaces in which they can
make a living, but where they also make themselves obtru-
sively and disturbingly visible, to off-limits spaces where
they can do neither. 'Prowlers', 'stalkers', 'loiterers',
'obtrusive beggars', 'travellers' and other kinds of tres-
passers have become the most sinister characters in the
nightmares of the elite.

As first suggested by Manuel Castells, there is a growing
polarization, and an ever more complete break in communication between the lifeworlds of the two categories into
which city residents are split:

> The space of the upper tier is usually connected to global
> communication and to a vast network of exchange, open to
> messages and experiences that embrace the entire world. At
> the other end of the spectrum, segmented local networks,
> often ethnically based, rely on their identity as the most
> valuable resource to defend their interests, and ultimately
> their being.[7]

The picture emerging from that description is one of two
segregated and mutually separate lifeworlds. Only the
second of the two is territorially circumscribed and can be
caught in the net sewn of orthodox topographical,
mundane and 'down to earth' notions. Those who live in
the first of the two distinct lifeworlds may be, like the
others, bodily '*in* the place', but they are not '*of* that place' –
certainly not spiritually, but also quite often, whenever they
wish, not bodily.

The 'upper tier' people do not belong to the place they
inhabit since their concerns lie (or rather float and drift)
elsewhere. One can guess that apart from being left
alone and so free to devote themselves fully to their own

pastimes, and to be assured of the services indispensable for daily comforts (however defined), they have no other interests vested in the city in which their residences are located. The city population is not their grazing ground, the source of their wealth and so also a ward in their custody, care and responsibility, as it used to be for the old urban elites of yore, the factory owners or the merchants of consumables and ideas. By and large, the present-day urban elites are *unconcerned* with the affairs of 'their' city, just one locality among many, all such localities being small and insignificant from the vantage point of cyberspace – their genuine, even if virtual, home. At least they need not be concerned, and apparently nothing can compel them to be concerned if they decide not to be.

The lifeworld of the other, 'lower' tier of city residents is the very opposite of the first. In a sharp contrast to the upper stratum, it is marked by being cut off from that worldwide network of communication to which the 'upper tier' people are connected and to which their lives are tuned. The lower-tier city dwellers are 'doomed to stay local' – and so one could and should expect their attention and concerns, complete with their discontents, dreams and hopes, to be focused on 'local affairs'. For them, it is *inside* the city they inhabit that the battle for survival and a decent place in the world is launched, waged and sometimes won, but mostly lost.

Of São Paulo, the second largest Brazilian city, bustling and expanding fast, Teresa Caldeira writes:

> São Paulo is today a city of walls. Physical barriers have been constructed everywhere – around houses, apartment buildings, parks, squares, office complexes and schools . . . A new aesthetics of security shapes all types of constructions and imposes new logic of surveillance and distance . . .[8]

Anyone who can afford it buys a residence in a 'condo-minium', intended as a hermitage physically inside the city but socially and spiritually outside it. 'Closed communities are supposed to be separate worlds. Their advertisements propose a "total way of life" which would represent an alternative to the quality of life offered by the city and its deteriorated public space.' The most prominent feature of the condominium is its 'isolation and distance from the city . . . Isolation means separation from those considered to be socially inferior', and as the developers and the real-estate agents insist, 'the key factor to assure this is security. This means fences and walls surrounding the condominium, guards on duty twenty-four hours a day controlling the entrances, and an array of facilities and services' 'for keeping the others out'.

As we all know, fences have to have two sides . . . Fences divide otherwise uniform space into an 'inside' and an 'outside', but what is 'inside' for those on one side of the fence is 'outside' for those on the other. The residents of condominiums fence themselves 'out' of the off-putting, discomfiting, vaguely threatening because hurly-burly and rough life of the city, and 'in' to an oasis of calm and safety. By the same token, though, they fence all the others out of the decent and secure places whose standards they are pre-pared and determined to keep up and defend tooth and nail, and into the self-same shabby and squalid streets which they try, no expense spared, to evade. The fence separates the 'voluntary ghetto' of the high and mighty from the many enforced ones of the down and out. For the insiders of the voluntary ghetto, the other ghettoes are spaces where 'we won't go'. For the insiders of the involuntary ones, the area to which they are confined (by being excluded from else-where) is the space 'we are not allowed to get out of'.

Let me restate the point from which our analysis started: originally constructed to provide safety for all its inhabitants, cities are associated these days more often with danger than they are with security. To quote Nan Ellin once more: 'the fear factor [in the construction and reconstruction of cities] has certainly grown, as indicated by the growth in locked car and house doors and security systems, the popularity of "gated" and "secure" communities for all age and income groups, and the increasing surveillance of public spaces, not to mention the unending reports of danger emitted by the mass media.'[9]

Genuine and putative threats to the body and the property of the individual are fast turning into major considerations whenever the merits or disadvantages of a place to live are contemplated. They have been also assigned the topmost position in real-estate marketing policy. Uncertainty about the future, frailty of social position, and existential insecurity – those ubiquitous accompaniments of life in a 'liquid modern' world notoriously rooted in remote places and so staying beyond individual control – tend to be focused on the nearest targets and channelled into concerns with personal safety; the kinds of concerns that are condensed in turn into segregationist/exclusionist urges, inexorably leading to urban space wars.

As we can learn from the perceptive study by Steven Flusty, an acute architectural/urbanistic critic, servicing that war, and particularly designing ways to bar access to claimed spaces against current, potential and putative malefactors, and keeping them at a safe distance, now constitutes the most rapidly expanding concern of architectural innovators and urban developers in American cities.[10] Novel urbanistic products, the ones most proudly advertised and widely imitated, are 'interdictory spaces', 'designed to intercept, repel or filter the would-be users'. Explicitly, the purpose of 'interdictory spaces' is to divide, segregate and exclude – not to build bridges, easy passages and meeting places, facilitate communication and otherwise bring the residents of the city together.

The architectural/urbanistic inventions listed by Flusty are the technically updated equivalents of the premodern moats, turrets and embrasures of the city walls; but rather than defending the city and all its dwellers against the enemy outside, they are erected to set and keep the various kinds of city residents apart from each other (and away from mischief) – and to defend some of them against the others, once they have been cast in the status of adversaries by the very act of spatial isolation. Among the varieties of 'interdictory spaces' named by Flusty, there is 'slippery space', 'space that cannot be reached, due to contorted, protracted, or missing paths of approach'; 'prickly space', 'space that cannot be comfortably occupied, defended by such details as wall-mounted sprinkler heads activated to clear loiterers or ledges sloped to inhibit sitting'; or 'jittery space', 'space that cannot be utilized unobserved due to active monitoring by roving patrols and/or remote technologies feeding to security stations'. These and other kinds of 'interdictory spaces' have but one – though composite – purpose: to cut the extraterritorial enclaves off from the continuous city territory; in other words, to erect compact little fortresses inside which the members of the supraterritorial global elite can groom, cultivate and relish their bodily, in addition to spiritual, independence and isolation from the locality. In the landscape of the city, 'interdictory spaces' have become landmarks of the *disintegration* of locally grounded, shared communal living.

The secession of the new elite (locally settled, but globally oriented and only loosely attached to its place of settlement) from its past engagement with the local populace, and the resulting spiritual/communication gap between the living/lived spaces of those who have seceded and those who have been left behind, are arguably the most seminal of the social, cultural and political departures associated with the passage from the 'solid' to the 'liquid' stage of modernity.

There is a lot of truth, and nothing but the truth, in that picture of mutual separation sketched above. But not the whole truth.

Among those parts of the truth which are missing or played down, the most significant accounts (more than any of the more notorious aspects) for arguably the most vital (and probably in the long run most consequential) characteristic of contemporary urban life: namely, the intimate interplay between globalizing pressures and the fashion in which the identities of urban sites are negotiated, formed and re-formed.

Contrary to what is ultimately suggested by the opting out of the 'upper tier', it would be a mistake to visualize the 'global' and the 'local' aspects of contemporary living conditions and life politics as residing in two separate and hermetically sealed spaces that only marginally and occasionally communicate. In his recently published study, Michael Peter Smith objects to the opinion (suggested in his view by, for instance, David Harvey or John Friedman)[11] that opposes 'a dynamic but placeless logic of global economic flows' to 'a static image of place and local culture', now 'valorized' as the 'life place' 'of being-in-the-world'.[12] In Smith's own opinion, 'far from reflecting a static ontology of "being" or "community", localities are dynamic constructions "in the making".'

Indeed, it is only in the ethereal world of theory that the line separating the abstract, 'somewhere in the nowhere' space of global operators from the fleshy, tangible, supremely 'here and now' space-within-reach of 'locals' can easily be drawn. The realities of city life will surely play havoc with such neat divisions. Drawing boundaries in lived space is a matter of continuous contention and a stake in the battles waged on numerous criss-crossing fronts; all drawings of a line are provisional and temporary, under threat of being redrawn or effaced, and for that reason they provide a natural outlet from the wide range of anxieties born of an insecure life. The sole lasting effect of the continuous yet vain efforts to fortify and stabilize the vexingly unstable boundaries is the recycling of diffuse fears into targeted prejudices, group antagonisms, occasional confrontations and perpetually simmering hostilities. Besides, no one in our fast globalizing world can truthfully claim to be a 'global operator' pure and simple. The most that the members of the globally influential and globe-trotting elite can manage is a wider scope for their mobility.

If things get too hot for comfort and the space around their city residences proves too hazardous and too difficult to manage, they may move elsewhere; they have an option not available to the rest of their (physically) close neighbours. The option to find a more agreeable alternative to local discomforts gives them a degree of independence of which other urban residents can only dream, and a luxury of lofty indifference those others cannot afford. Their interest in, and their commitment to 'putting the city's affairs in order' tend to be considerably less comprehensive and unconditional than in the case of those who have less freedom unilaterally to break the local bond.

All that does not mean, however, that in their search for 'meaning and identity', which they need and crave no less intensely than the next person, the globally connected elite can leave out of account the place in which they (even if temporarily and 'until further notice') live and work. Like all other men and women, they can't help being a part of the cityscape, and their life pursuits are inscribed willy-nilly in the locality. As global operators, they may roam cyberspace; but as human agents, they are confined day in day out to the physical space in which they operate, to the environment pre-set and continually reprocessed in the course of the struggles of human beings for meaning, identity and recognition. It is around *places* that human experience tends to be formed and gleaned, that life-sharing is attempted to be managed, that life meanings are conceived, absorbed and negotiated. And it is *in* places that human urges and desires are gestated and incubated, that they live in the hope of fulfilment, run the risk of frustration – and are indeed, more often than not, frustrated and strangled.

Contemporary cities are for that reason the stages or battlegrounds on which global powers and stubbornly local meanings and identities meet, clash, struggle and seek a satisfactory, or just bearable, settlement – a mode of cohabitation that is hoped to be a lasting peace but as a rule proves to be only an armistice; brief intervals to repair broken defences and redeploy fighting units. It is that confrontation, and not any single factor, that sets in motion and guides the dynamics of the 'liquid modern' city.

And let there be no mistake: this can be *any* city, even if not every one to the same degree. On his recent trip to Copenhagen, Michael Peter Smith recalls walking in a single hour 'past small groups of Turkish, African, and Middle Eastern immigrants', observing 'several veiled and unveiled Arab women', reading 'signs in various non-European languages', and having 'an interesting conversation with an Irish bartender, in an English pub, across from Tivoli Garden'.[13] These field experiences proved to be helpful, says Smith, in the talk on transnational connections he gave in Copenhagen later in the week, 'when a questioner insisted that transnationalism was a phenomenon that might apply to "global cities" like New York or London, but had little relevance to more insular places like Copenhagen'.

The real powers that shape the conditions under which we all act these days flow in *global* space, while our institutions of political action remain by and large tied to the ground; they are, as before, *local*.

Because they are now and are bound to stay for the foreseeable future mainly local, the political agencies which operate in the urban space, on the stage where the drama of politics is performed daily, tend to be fatally afflicted with a grave insufficiency of the power to act, and particularly of the kind of power that would allow them to act effectively and in a sovereign manner. The flip side of that relative disempowerment of local politics is the dearth of politics in extraterritorial cyberspace, that playground of real power.

One of the most bewildering paradoxes revealed in our time is that on the fast *globalizing* planet politics tends to be passionately and self-consciously *local*. Evicted from, or rather never admitted to and still barred access to cyberspace, it falls back and rebounds on affairs 'within reach': on local matters and neighbourhood relations. For most of us and for most of the time, local issues seem to be *the only* ones we can 'do something about' – influence, repair, improve, redirect. It is only in local matters that our actions or inaction can be credited with 'making a difference', since for the state of those other 'supralocal' affairs there is (or so we are repeatedly told by our political leaders and all other 'people in the know') 'no alternative'; we come to suspect that, given the pitifully inadequate means and resources at our disposal, 'global affairs' will take their course whatever we do or whatever we can sensibly contemplate doing.

But even if their recondite roots and causes are undoubtedly *global* and far away, matters enter the realm of political concerns solely through their *local* offshoots and repercussions. The global pollution of air or water supplies – much like the global production of 'redundant' people and exiles – turns into a matter for *politics* when a dumping ground for toxic waste, or housing for homeless refugees and asylum seekers, is allocated next door to us, in 'our own backyard', in frighteningly close, but also encouragingly 'within reach', proximity to our homestead. The progressive commercialization of health concerns, obviously an effect of throat-cutting competition between supranational pharmaceutical giants, comes into *political* view when the services of a neighbourhood hospital are run down or the local old people's homes and mental care institutions are phased out. It was the residents of one city, New York, or even of Manhattan, just one part of that sprawling city, who had to cope with the havoc caused by globally gestated terrorism; and it is the councils and mayors of other cities who now have to assume responsibility for the protection of individual safety, newly vulnerable and exposed to forces securely entrenched far beyond the reach of any municipality, and delivering blows from the security of their faraway shelters. Whereas the global devastation of livelihoods and the uprooting of long settled populations enter the horizon of political action through the tasks of integrating the colourful 'economic migrants' crowding the once uniform looking streets . . .

To cut a long story short: *cities have become dumping grounds for globally conceived and gestated problems.* The residents of cities and their elected representatives tend to be confronted with a task which by no stretch of imagination can they fulfil: the task of finding *local* solutions to *globally conceived* troubles and quandaries.

Hence, let me repeat, arises the paradox of an increasingly local politics in a world increasingly shaped and reshaped by global processes. As noted by Castells, the ever more conspicuous mark of our time is the intense (one might say compulsive and increasingly obsessive)

'production of meaning and identity: my neighbourhood, my community, my city, my school, my tree, my
river, my beach, my chapel, my peace, my environment'.[14]
'Defenceless against the global whirlwind, people stick to
themselves.' And let me note that the more they 'stick to
themselves', the more 'defenceless against the global
whirlwind' they tend to become, and so also less capable
of deciding, let alone asserting, the local, ostensibly their
own, meanings and identities – to the great joy of global
operators, who have no reason to fear the defenceless.

As Castells implies elsewhere, the creation of the 'space
of flows' sets a new (global) hierarchy of domination-
through-the-threat-of-disengagement. The 'space of flows'
can 'escape the control of any locale', while (and because!)
'the space of places is fragmented, localized, and thus
increasingly powerless vis-à-vis the versatility of the space of
flows, with the only chance of resistance for localities being
to refuse landing rights for overwhelming flows – only to see
that they land in the locale nearby, inducing therefore the
bypassing and marginalization of rebellious communities.'[15]

As a result, *local politics* – and particularly *urban* politics –
has become hopelessly overloaded far beyond its carrying and
performing capacity. It is now expected to mitigate the consequences of a globalization running out of control, while
using means and resources that that self-same globalization
has rendered pitifully inadequate. Hence the perpetual
uncertainty under which all political agents are obliged to
act; an uncertainty which the politicians sometimes
acknowledge, but most of the time try to cover up by a
public display of muscle-flexing and rhetorical bravado
that tends to be more vigorous and vociferous the more
hapless and short-handed the politicians themselves are.

Whatever has happened to the cities in their history and
however drastically their spatial structure, look and lifestyle

may have changed over the years or centuries, one feature has remained constant: cities are spaces where *strangers* stay and move in close proximity to one another.

Being a permanent component of city life, the perpetual and ubiquitous presence of strangers within sight and reach adds a good measure of perpetual uncertainty to all of the city dwellers' life pursuits. That presence, impossible to avoid for more than a brief moment, is a never-drying source of anxiety and of an aggression that is usually dormant, yet erupts time and again.

The ambient, if subliminal, fear of the unknown desperately seeks credible outlets. On most occasions, the accumulated anxieties tend to be unloaded against a selected category of 'aliens', chosen to epitomize 'strangeness': the unfamiliarity and opacity of the life-setting, the vagueness of risks and the unknown nature of threats. By chasing a selected category of 'aliens' away from their homes and shops, the frightening ghost of uncertainty is, for a time, exorcised; the horrifying monster of insecurity is burnt in effigy. The latent function of the barriers at the border, ostensibly erected against 'false asylum seekers' and 'merely economic' migrants, is to fortify the shaky, erratic and unpredictable existence of the insiders. But liquid modern life is bound to stay erratic and capricious whatever the treatment given and whatever plight is visited on 'undesirable aliens' – and so the relief tends to be short-lived, and the hopes attached to 'tough and decisive measures' are dashed as soon as they are raised.

The stranger is, by definition, an agent moved by intentions that one can at best guess, while never being sure of having grasped them in full. The stranger is the unknown variable in all equations whenever decisions calculating what to do and how to behave are pondered by city residents; and so even if the strangers do not become objects of overt aggression and are not openly and actively resented, their presence inside the field of action remains discomfiting, making a tall order of the task of predicting the effects of actions and the chances of their success or failure.

Sharing space with strangers, living in the unsolicited yet obtrusive proximity of strangers, is a condition that city residents find difficult, perhaps impossible to escape. The proximity of strangers is their fate, a permanent modus vivendi which must be daily scrutinized and monitored, experimented with, tested and retested, and (hopefully) put into a shape that will make cohabitation with strangers palatable and life in their company liveable. That need is a 'given', non-negotiable; but the way in which city residents go about meeting its demands is a matter of choice. And some sort of choice is made daily – whether by commission or omission, design or default; by conscious decision or just by following, blindly and mechanically, the customary patterns; by joint discussion and deliberation, or just through following individually the currently trusted (because currently fashionable and not yet discredited) means.

The developments described by Steven Flusty and quoted above are high-tech manifestations of an ubiquitous urban *mixophobia*.

'Mixophobia' is a highly predictable and widespread reaction to the mind-boggling, spine-chilling and nerve-breaking variety of human types and lifestyles that meet and rub elbows and shoulders in the streets of contemporary cities not only in the officially proclaimed (and for that reason avoided) 'rough districts' or 'mean streets', but in their 'ordinary' (read: unprotected by 'interdictory spaces') living areas. As the polyvocality and cultural variegation of the urban environment of the globalization era sets in, likely to intensify rather than be mitigated in the course of time, the tensions arising from the vexing/confusing/irritating unfamiliarity of the setting will probably go on prompting segregationist urges.

Unloading such urges may (temporarily, yet repeatedly) relieve rising tensions. Each successive offload renews the hope frustrated by the one before: that, even if the off-putting and disconcerting differences prove unassailable and intractable, perhaps at least the poison may be squeezed out of their stings by assigning to each form of life its separate, inclusive as well as exclusive, well-marked and well-guarded physical spaces . . . Meanwhile, short of that radical solution, perhaps one could at least secure for oneself, for one's kith and kin and other 'people like oneself', a territory free from that jumble and mess that irredeemably afflicts other city areas. Mixophobia manifests itself in the drive towards islands of similarity and sameness amidst the sea of variety and difference.

The roots of mixophobia are banal, not at all difficult to locate, easy to understand though not necessarily easy to forgive. As Richard Sennett suggests, 'the "we" feeling, which expresses a desire to be similar, is a way for men' and women 'to avoid the necessity of looking deeper into each other'.[16] It promises, we may say, some spiritual comfort: the prospect of making togetherness easier to bear by cutting off that effort to understand, to negotiate, to compromise that living amidst and with difference requires. 'Innate to the process of forming a coherent image of community is the desire to avoid actual participation. Feeling common bonds without common experience occurs in the first place because men are afraid of participation, afraid of the dangers and the challenges of it, afraid of its pain.'

The drive towards a 'community of similarity' is a sign of withdrawal not just from the otherness *outside*, but also from commitment to the lively yet turbulent, invigorating yet cumbersome interaction *inside*. The attraction of a 'community of sameness' is that of an insurance policy against the risks with which daily life in a polyvocal world is fraught. An immersion in 'sameness' does not decrease, let alone stave off the risks that prompted it. Like all palliatives, it may at most promise only a shelter from some of their most immediate and most feared effects.

Choosing the escape option as the medicine for mixophobia has an insidious and deleterious consequence of its own: once adopted, the allegedly therapeutic regime becomes self-perpetuating and self-reinforcing the more ineffective it is. Sennett explains why this is (indeed, must be) the case: 'Cities in America during the past two decades have grown in such a way that ethnic areas become relatively homogeneous; it appears no accident that the fear of the outsider has also grown to the extent that these ethnic communities have been cut off.'[17] The longer people stay in a uniform environment – in the company of others 'like them' with whom they can 'socialize' perfunctorily and matter-of-factly without incurring the risk of miscomprehension and without struggling with the vexing need to translate between distinct universes of meaning – the more they are likely to 'unlearn' the art of negotiating shared meanings and an agreeable modus covivendi. Since they have forgotten or neglected to acquire the skills necessary for a gratifying life amidst difference, there is little wonder that the seekers and practitioners of escape therapy view the prospect of confronting the strangers face-to-face with rising horror. Strangers tend to appear ever more frightening as they become increasingly alien, unfamiliar and incomprehensible, and as the dialogue and interaction which could eventually have assimilated their 'otherness' to one's own lifeworld fade, or fail to take off in the first place. The drive towards a homogeneous, territorially isolated environment may be triggered by mixophobia; but *practising* territorial separation is that mixophobia's lifebelt and food purveyor; it turns gradually into its principal reinforcement.

Mixophobia, though, is not the sole combatant on the urban battlefield.

City living is a notoriously ambivalent experience. It attracts *and* repels. To make the plight of the city dweller still more harrowing and difficult to repair, it is *the same* aspects of city life that, intermittently or simultaneously, attract and repel . . . The confusing variety of the urban environment is a source of fear (particularly for those among us who have already 'lost the familiar ways', having been cast into a state of acute uncertainty by the destabilizing processes of globalization). *The same* kaleidoscope-like twinkle and glimmer of the urban scenery, however never short of novelty and surprise, constitutes its difficult-to-resist charm and seductive power.

Confronting the never-stopping and constantly dazzling spectacle of the city is not therefore experienced unambiguously as a bane and a curse; nor is sheltering from it felt as a pure blessing. The city prompts *mixophilia* as much as it sows and feeds mixophobia. Intrinsically and irreparably, city life is an *ambivalent* affair.

The bigger and more heterogeneous a city, the more attractions it may support and offer. The massive condensation of strangers is, simultaneously, a repellent and a most powerful magnet, drawing to the city ever new cohorts of men and women weary of the monotony of rural or small-town life, fed up with its repetitive routines – and despairing of the prospect-less dearth of chances. Variety is a promise of opportunities, many and different opportunities, opportunities fitting all skills and any taste – and so the bigger the city the more likely it is to attract a growing number of people who reject or are denied opportunities and chances of adventure in places that are smaller and so less tolerant of idiosyncrasy and more close-fisted in the liberties they offer or indeed tolerate. It seems that mixophilia, just like mixophobia, is a self-propelling, self-propagating and self-invigorating tendency. Neither of the two is likely to exhaust itself, or lose any of its vigour in the course of city renewal and the refurbishment of city space.

Mixophobia and mixophilia coexist in every city, but they coexist as well inside every one of the city's residents. Admittedly, this is an uneasy coexistence, full of sound and fury – though signifying a lot to the people on the receiving end of liquid modern ambivalence.

Since strangers are bound to carry on their lives in each other's company for a long time to come, whatever the future twists and turns of urban history, the art of living peacefully and happily with difference and benefiting from the variety of stimuli and opportunities acquires paramount importance among the skills a city resident needs to (and would be better to) learn and deploy.

Given the rising human mobility of the liquid modern epoch and the accelerated changes in the cast, plots and settings of the urban scene, the complete eradication of mixophobia does not seem to be on the cards. Perhaps something can be done, however, to influence the proportions in which mixophilia and mixophobia are mixed and to reduce the confusing impact of mixophobia, and the anxiety and anguish it generates. Indeed, it seems that architects and urban planners could do quite a lot to assist the growth of mixophilia and minimize the occasions for mixophobic responses to the challenges of city life. And there seems to be a lot that they can do and indeed are doing to facilitate the opposite effects.

As we have seen before, the segregation of residential areas and publicly attended spaces, however commercially attractive it may be to developers as a fast way of making profits, and attractive to their clients as a fast fix for mixophobia-generated anxieties, is in fact mixophobia's prime cause. The solutions on offer create or even aggravate the problems they claim to resolve: builders of gated communities and closely guarded condominiums, and the architects of 'interdictory spaces' create, reproduce and intensify the demand they claim to gratify and the need they promise to fulfil.

Mixophobic paranoia feeds upon itself and acts as a self-fulfilling prophecy. If segregation is offered and taken up as a radical cure for the dangers represented by strangers, cohabitation with strangers becomes more difficult by the day. Homogenizing living quarters and then reducing to an unavoidable minimum all commerce and communication between them is a foolproof recipe for intensifying and deepening the urge to exclude and segregate. Such a measure may temporarily help to reduce the pains suffered by people afflicted with mixophobia, but the cure is itself pathogenic and makes the affliction deeper and less curable, so that ever new and stronger doses of the medicine are needed to keep the pain at a tolerably low level. The social homogeneity of space, emphasized and fortified by spatial segregation, lowers tolerance to difference in its residents and so multiplies the occasions for mixophobic reactions, making city life look more 'risk-prone' and so more agonizing, rather than making it feel more secure and so more easy-going and enjoyable.

More favourable to the entrenchment and cultivation of mixophiliac sentiments would be the opposite architectural and urban planning strategy: the propagation of open, inviting and hospitable public spaces which all categories of urban residents would be tempted to attend regularly and knowingly and willingly share. As Hans Gadamer famously pointed out in his *Truth and Method*, mutual understanding is prompted by a 'fusion of horizons': the cognitive horizons, that is, the horizons drawn and expanded in the course of the accumulation of life experience. The 'fusion' that mutual understanding requires can only be the outcome of *shared* experience; and sharing experience is inconceivable without shared space.

The most harrowing contemporary fears are born of existential uncertainty. Their roots reach well beyond urban living conditions, and whatever might be done inside the city and at the scale of city space and city-managed resources to cut those roots will stop well short of what that undertaking would require. The mixophobia haunting the cohabitation of city residents is not the source of their anxiety, but a product of a perverse and misleading interpretation of its sources; a manifestation of desperate attempts, in the end inconclusive, to mitigate the pain that anxiety inflicts – by removing the rash while mistaking it for the cure of the illness. It is mixophilia, as ingrained in city life as its mixophobic opposition, that carries a germ of hope: not only the hope of making urban living – a kind of living that calls for cohabitation and interaction with an enormous, perhaps infinite variety of strangers – less worrying and easier to practise, but also the hope of mitigating the tensions arising, from similar causes, at the planetary scale.

As mentioned before, nowadays cities are dumping grounds for globally produced troubles; but they may also be seen as laboratories in which the ways and means of living with difference, still to be learned by the residents of an increasingly overcrowded planet, are daily invented, put to the test, memorized and assimilated. The work of Gadamer's 'fusion of horizons', that necessary condition of Kant's *allgemeine Vereinigung der Menschheit*, may well begin on the urban stage. On that stage Huntington's apocalyptic vision of the irreconcilable conflict and inescapable 'clash of civilizations'[18] can be translated into benign, and often deeply gratifying and enjoyable daily encounters with the humanity hiding behind the frighteningly unfamiliar scenic masks of different and mutually alien races, nationalities, gods and liturgies. Nowhere more than on the shared city streets can one discover and learn that, as Mark Juergensmeyer has put it,[19] though 'secular ideological expressions of rebellion' tend these days to be 'replaced by ideological formulations that are religious', 'the grievances – the sense of alienation, marginalization, and social frustration – are often much the same' across all the separating and antagonizing denominational borders.

5

Utopia in the Age of Uncertainty

The lives of even the happiest people among us (or, by a common and somewhat envy-tainted opinion of the unhappy, the luckiest) are anything but trouble-free. Few of us are ready to declare that everything in their life works as they would like it to work – and even those few know moments of doubt.

We are all familiar with unpleasant and uncomfortable occasions when things or people cause us worries we would not expect them, and certainly not wish them, to cause. What makes such adversities ('blows of fate', as we sometimes call them) particularly irksome is that they fall unannounced – we do not expect them to come, and quite often will not believe that they might be near. They hit us, as we say, 'like bolts out of the blue' – so we can't take precautions and avert the catastrophe, since no one expects a thunderbolt from a cloudless sky . . .

The suddenness of the blows, their irregularity, their nasty ability to appear from any direction – all that makes them unpredictable, and us defenceless. As long as dangers remain eminently free-floating, freakish and frivolous, we are their sitting targets – there is pretty little we can do, if anything at all, to prevent them. Such hopelessness is frightening. Uncertainty means fear. No wonder we dream, time and again, of a world with no accidents. A regular world. A predictable world. Not a poker-faced world; even if some philosophers, like Leibniz, are right when they argue that even a 'perfect world' would not be perfect if it did not contain some measure of evil, at least let that evil be confined to enclosures that are reliably fenced off, well mapped and closely watched and guarded, so that one can know what is what, what is where and when one should expect something to happen – and be ready to meet it when it comes. To put it in a nutshell, we dream of a reliable world, one we can trust. A secure world.

'Utopia' is the name which, courtesy of Sir Thomas More, has commonly been given to such dreams since the sixteenth century; that is, since the time when the old and apparently timeless routines began to fall apart, when old habits and conventions started to show their age and rituals their seediness, when violence became rife (or that it was how people tended to explain the profusion of unorthodox demands and actions they were not accustomed to, and which the powers they had heretofore believed to be omnipotent found too unruly and/or too unwieldy to be held in check, and too potent and intractable to be tamed in the old and apparently tested ways). When Sir Thomas More penned his blueprint for a world free from unpredictable threats, improvisation and experimentation fraught with risks and errors were fast becoming the order of the day.

Sir Thomas knew only too well that as much as it was a design for the setting of the good life, his blueprint for a world cleansed of insecurity and unanchored fears was only a dream: he called that blueprint 'utopia', hinting simultaneously at *two* Greek words: *eutopia*, that is 'good place', and *outopia*, which meant 'nowhere'. His numerous followers and imitators, however, were more resolute or less cautious. They lived in a world already confident, rightly or wrongly and for better or worse, that it had the sagacity needed to design a preferable, fear-free world, and the acumen required to lift the unreasonable 'is' to the level of the reason-dictated 'ought'. That confidence gave them the courage and the gumption to try both.

For the next few centuries, the modern world was to be an optimistic world; a world-living-towards-utopia. It was also to be a world believing that a society without utopia is not liveable, and consequently a life without utopia is not worth living. If in doubt, one could always rely on the authority of the brightest and most adored minds around. For instance, on Oscar Wilde:

> A map of the world that does not include Utopia is not worth even glancing at, for it leaves out the one country at which Humanity is always landing. And when Humanity lands there, it looks out, and seeing a better country, sets sail. Progress is the realization of Utopias.

With the benefit of a hindsight, one is inclined to correct the last sentence, though – and this on two accounts. First, progress was a *chase after utopias*, rather than their *realization*. Utopias played the role of a dummy rabbit – ferociously pursued but never caught by racing dogs. And second: most of the time, the movement called 'progress' was more an effort to run away from failed utopias than an effort to catch up with utopias not yet experienced; a run away from the 'not as good as expected', rather than a run from the 'good' to the 'better'; an effort spurred by past frustrations rather than by future bliss. Realities declared to be 'realizations' of utopias were more often than not found to be ugly caricatures of dreams, and not the dreamt-of paradise. The overwhelming reason to 'set sail' again was an aversion to what *had been* done, rather than the attraction of what *might yet be* done . . .

From across the Channel came an opinion which chimed well with that of Oscar Wilde, set down by another wise man, Anatole France:

> Without the Utopias of other times, men would still live in caves, miserable and naked. It was Utopians who traced the lines of the first city . . . Out of generous dreams come beneficial realities. Utopia is the principle of all progress, and the essay into a better future.

Evidently, at the time of Anatole France's birth, utopias had settled so firmly into public awareness and the pursuits of day-to-day life that human existence *without* utopia appeared to the French writer to be not only inferior and terminally flawed, but downright unimaginable. It seemed obvious to Anatole France, as it did to many of his contemporaries, that even the troglodytes had to dream their utopias so that we might no longer live in caves . . . How indeed, Anatole France would ask, could we otherwise be able to stroll along Baron Haussmann's Parisian boulevards? There could be no 'first city' unless the 'utopia of a city' had preceded its building! At all times we tend to project our own way of life onto other life forms if we wish to understand them – and so, to the generations tutored and groomed to be pulled by as yet untested utopias and pushed by already discredited ones, such a question would have seemed purely rhetorical, and its truth all but pleonastic . . .

And yet, contrary to the opinion voiced by Anatole France and grounded in his contemporaries' common sense, utopias were born together with modernity and only in the modern atmosphere were they able to breathe.

First and foremost, a utopia is an image of another universe, different from the universe one knows or knows of. In addition, it anticipates a universe originated entirely by human wisdom and devotion. But the idea that human beings can replace the world-that-is with another and different world, a world entirely of their own making, was almost wholly absent from human thought before the advent of modern times.

The grindingly monotonous self-reproduction of premodern forms of human life, subject only to changes too sluggish to be noted, gave little inspiration and even less encouragement to ruminations on alternative forms of human life on earth, except in the shape of apocalypses or the last judgment, both of them of divine provenance. To take the human imagination to the drawing board at which the first utopias were sketched, an accelerating collapse of the human world's self-reproductive capacity was needed; a kind of collapse that went down in history as the birth of the modern era.

To be born, the utopian dream needed two conditions. First, an overwhelming (even if diffuse and as yet inarticulate) feeling that the world was not functioning properly and was unlikely to be set right without a thorough overhaul. Second, the confidence in human potency to rise to the task, a belief that 'we, humans, can do it', armed as we are with reason which can spy out what is wrong with the world and find out what to use in replacing its diseased parts, as well as with an ability to construct the tools and weapons required for grafting such designs onto human reality. In short, confidence was needed that under human management the world could be put into a shape more suitable for the satisfaction of human needs – whatever those needs already were or might yet become.

We may say that if the premodern posture towards the world was akin to that of a gamekeeper, it was the gardener's attitude that would best serve as a metaphor for the modern worldview and practice.

The main task of a gamekeeper is to defend the land assigned to his wardenship against all human interference, in order to defend and preserve, so to speak, its 'natural balance', that incarnation of God's or Nature's infinite wisdom. The gamekeeper's task is promptly to discover and disable the snares set by poachers and to prevent alien, illegitimate hunters from trespassing – lest the perpetuation of that 'natural balance' be jeopardized. The gamekeeper's services rest on the belief that things are at their best when they are not tinkered with; in premodern times they rested on the belief that the world was a divine chain of being in which every creature had its rightful and useful place, even if human mental abilities were too limited to comprehend the wisdom, harmony and orderliness of God's design.

Not so the gardener; he assumes that there would be no order in the world at all (or at least in the small part of that world entrusted to his wardenship) were it not for his constant attention and effort. The gardener knows better what kinds of plants should, and what sorts of plants should not grow in the plot under his care. He first works out the desirable arrangement in his head, and then sees to it that this image is engraved on the plot. He forces his preconceived design on the plot by encouraging the growth of the right types of plants (mostly the plants he himself has sown or planted) and uprooting and destroying all other plants, now renamed 'weeds', whose uninvited and unwanted presence, unwanted *because* uninvited, can't be squared with the overall harmony of the design.

It is the gardeners who tend to be the most keen and expert (one is tempted to say, professional) utopia-makers. It is at the gardeners' image of ideal harmony, first laid out in blueprint in their heads, that 'the gardens always land', a prototype for the way in which humanity, to recall Oscar Wilde's postulate, would tend to land in the country called 'utopia'.

If one hears today phrases like 'the demise of utopia', or 'the end of utopia', or 'the fading of the utopian imagination', sprinkled over contemporary debates densely enough to take root in common sense and so be taken as self-evident, it is because the posture of the gardener is nowadays giving way to that of the *hunter*.

Unlike the two types that happened to prevail before his tenure started, the hunter could not care less about the overall 'balance of things', whether 'natural' or designed and contrived. The sole task hunters pursue is another 'kill', big enough to fill their game-bags to capacity. Most certainly, they would not consider it to be their duty to make sure that the supply of game roaming in the forest will be replenished after (and despite) their hunt. If the woods have been emptied of game due to a particularly profitable escapade, hunters may move to another relatively unspoiled wilderness, still teeming with would-be hunting trophies. It may occur to them that sometime, in a distant and still undefined future, the planet might run out of undepleted forests; but if it does, they wouldn't see it as an immediate worry – and certainly not as *their* worry. Such a distant prospect will not after all jeopardize the results of the current hunt, or the next one, and so surely there is nothing in it to oblige me, just one single hunter among many, or us, just one single hunting association among many, to ponder, let alone do something about it.

We are all hunters now, or told to be hunters and called or compelled to act as hunters do, on penalty of eviction from hunting, if not (perish the thought!) of relegation to the ranks of the game. And whenever we look around, we are likely mostly to see other lonely hunters like us, or hunters hunting in packs the way we also occasionally try to do. And we would need to try really hard before we could spot a gardener who was contemplating some predesigned harmony beyond the fence of his private garden and then went out to bring it about (that relative rarity of gardeners and the growing profusion of hunters is what social scientists discuss under the learned name of 'individualization'). We certainly won't find many gamekeepers, or even hunters with the rudiments of the gamekeeper's worldview – this being the prime reason why people with an 'ecological conscience' are alarmed and try their best to alert the rest of us (that slow yet steady extinction of gamekeeper-style philosophy combined with a waning of its gardener-style variety is what politicians extol under the name of 'deregulation').

It stands to reason that in a world populated mostly by hunters there is little if any room left for utopian musings; and that not many people are likely to treat utopian blueprints seriously, were someone to offer one to them for their consideration. And so, even if one knew how to make the world better and took the task of making it better to heart, the truly puzzling question will be: who has sufficient resources and a strong enough will to do what needs to be done . . .

The expectation of such resourcefulness and such a will to act used to be vested in the sovereign authority of nation-states, but as Jacques Attali recently observed in *La Voie humaine*, 'nations have lost influence on the course of affairs and have abandoned to the forces of globalization all means of guiding the world towards a destination, and of mounting a defence against all varieties of fear.' And the 'forces of globalization' which have taken many of the nation-state's former powers are hardly notorious for their 'gamekeeping' or 'gardening' instincts, philosophies or strategies. They favour hunting and hunters instead.

As a reference book for hunters, Roget's Thesaurus, justly acclaimed for its faithful recording of successive changes in verbal usage, now seems to have every right to list the concept of the 'utopian' in close proximity to 'fanci-ful', 'fantastic', 'fictional', 'chimerical', 'air-built', 'imprac-tical', 'unrealistic', 'unreasonable' and 'irrational'. And so are we perhaps indeed witnessing the end of utopia?

I suppose that if utopia had a tongue and in addition was blessed with Mark Twain's wit, it would probably insist that reports of its death have been somewhat exagger-ated . . . And it would have good reason to say so. I typed the word 'utopia' a moment ago on my computer, and the Google searching machine has returned 4,400,000 web-sites (probably it will have added many more by the time you read these words); an impressive number even by notoriously excessive internet standards, and hardly a symptom of a putrefying corpse or even of a body in ter-minal convulsions.

Let us have a closer look, however, at the websites listed. The first on the list and arguably the most impressive informs surfers that 'Utopia is one of the largest free inter-active online games in the world – with over 80,000 players'. Then, scattered here and there, there are some references to the history of utopian ideas and to centres offering courses in that history, catering mostly for lovers of antiques and collectors of curiosities – the most common references among them going back to Sir Thomas More himself, the forefather of the whole thing. However, between them such websites constitute a minor-ity of entries.

I will not pretend that I browsed through all 4,400,000 entries (an intention to do so might perhaps be listed among the most utopian of the utopian projects), but the impression I received after reading a statistically decent random sample is that the term 'utopia' has mostly been appropriated by holiday, interior design and cosmetics companies, as well as by fashion houses. The websites have something in common: all of them offer *individual* services to individuals seeking *individual* satisfaction and *individual* escape from *individually* suffered discomforts.

And another impression I got: on the rare occasion when the word 'progress' appears on the homepages of such commercial websites, it no longer refers to a *forward drive*. Rather than a chase after a target spinning along, it implies a threat that makes a lucky escape imperative; it inspires the urge to *run away* from a disaster breathing down your neck . . .

'Utopia' used to denote a coveted, dreamt-of distant goal to which progress should, could and would eventually bring the seekers after a world better serving human needs. In contemporary dreams, however, the image of 'progress' seems to have moved from the discourse of *shared improvement* to that of *individual survival*. Progress is no longer thought about in the context of an urge to rush ahead, but in connection with a desperate effort to stay in the race. Awareness of progress makes one wary and calls for vigilance: hearing of 'times marching on', we tend to worry about being left behind, about falling over board from a fast accelerating vehicle, about finding no place in the next round of the game of 'musical chairs'. When you read, for instance, that Brazil is 'the only winter sun destination *this* winter', what you learn is that in the coming winter you must avoid being seen where people with aspirations similar to yours were bound to be seen *last* winter. Or you might read that you must 'lose the ponchos' which were so much *en vogue* last year, since time marches on and now you are told that wearing a poncho makes 'you look like a camel'. Or you will learn that donning pinstripe jackets and T-shirts – so 'must wear' and 'must be seen wearing' last season – is over, simply because 'any nobody' parades in them now. And so it goes on. Time flows on, and the trick is to keep pace with the waves. If you don't want to sink, keep surfing, and that means changing your wardrobe, your furnishings, your wallpaper, your look, your habits – in short, yourself – as often as you can manage it.

I don't need to add, since this should be obvious, that this new emphasis on the disposal of things, on abandoning them, getting rid of them, instead of on their appropriation well suits the logic of our consumer-oriented economy. People sticking to yesterday's clothes, computers, mobiles, or cosmetics would spell disaster for an economy whose main concern, and the condition *sine qua non* of its survival, is a rapid and accelerating assignment of sold and purchased products to waste; and in this economy swift disposal of waste is the cutting-edge industry.

Increasingly, *escape* now becomes the name of the most popular game in town. Semantically, escape is the very opposite of utopia, but psychologically it is, under present circumstances, its sole available substitute: one might say its new, updated and state-of-the-art rendition, refashioned to the measure of our deregulated, individualized society of consumers. You can no longer seriously hope to make *the world* a better place to live in; you can't even make really secure that better *place* in the world which you may have managed to carve out for yourself. Insecurity is here to stay, whatever happens. More than anything else, 'good luck' means keeping 'bad luck' at a distance.

What is left for your concerns and efforts, and having to attract most of your attention and powers, is the fight against *losing*: try at least to stay among the *hunters*, since the only alternative is to find yourself among the *hunted*. To be performed properly and with a chance of success, the fight against losing will require your full, undivided attention, vigilance twenty-four hours a day and seven days a week, and above all keeping on the move – as fast as you can . . .

Joseph Brodsky, the Russian-American philosopher-poet, vividly described the kind of life that has been set in motion and prompted by the compulsion to escape. The lot of the acknowledged losers, of the poor eliminated from the consumerist game, is a life of sporadic rebellion but more commonly of drug addiction: 'In general, a man shooting heroin into his vein does so largely for the same reason you buy a video,' Brodsky told the students of Dartmouth College in July 1989. As to the potential haves, which the Dartmouth College students aspire to become,

you'll be bored with your work, your spouses, your lovers, the view from your window, the furniture or wallpaper in your room, your thoughts, yourselves. Accordingly, you'll try to devise ways of escape. Apart from the self-gratifying gadgets mentioned before, you may take up changing jobs, residence, company, country, climate, you may take up promiscuity, alcohol, travel, cooking lessons, drugs, psychoanalysis . . .

In fact, you may lump all these together, and for a while that may work. Until the day, of course, when you wake up in your bedroom amid a new family and a different wallpaper, in a different state and climate, with a heap of bills from your travel agent and your shrink, yet with the same stale feeling toward the light of day pouring through your window . . .

Andrzej Stasiuk, an outstanding Polish novelist and a particularly perceptive analyst of the contemporary human condition, suggests that 'the possibility of becoming someone else' is the present-day substitute for the now largely discarded and uncared-for salvation or redemption.

Applying various techniques, we may change our bodies and reshape them according to different patterns . . . When browsing through glossy magazines, one gets the impression that they mostly tell one story – about the ways in which one can remake one's personality, starting from diets, surroundings, homes, and up to a rebuilding of our psychical structure, often code-named a proposition to 'be yourself'.

Sławomir Mrożek, a Polish writer of worldwide fame with first-hand experience of many lands and cultures, agrees with Stasiuk's hypothesis: 'In old times, when we felt unhappy, we accused God, then the world's manager; we assumed that He did not run the business properly. So we fired Him and appointed ourselves the new directors.' But – as Mrożek, a committed free-thinker loathing clerics and everything clerical, finds out – business did not improve with the change of management. It did not because when the dream and hope of a better life is fully focused on our own egos and reduced to tinkering with our own bodies or souls,

> there is no limit to our ambition and temptation to make that ego grow ever bigger, but first of all to refuse to accept any limits . . . I was told: 'invent yourself, invent your own life and manage it as you wish, in every single moment and from beginning to end.' But am I able to rise to such a task? With no help, trials, fittings, errors and rehashings, and above all without doubts?

The pain which used to be caused by unduly limited choice has now been replaced by no less a pain – though this time the pain is caused by an obligation to choose without trusting the choices made and without confidence that further choices will bring the target any closer. Mrożek compares the world we inhabit to a

> market-stall filled with fancy dresses and surrounded by crowds seeking their 'selves' . . . One can change dresses without end,

so what a wondrous liberty the seekers enjoy. . . . Let's go on searching for our real selves, it's smashing fun – on condition that the real self will never be found. Because if it were, the fun would end . . .

The dream of making uncertainty less daunting and happiness more permanent by changing one's ego, and of changing one's ego by changing its dresses, is the 'utopia' of hunters – a 'deregulated', 'privatized' and 'individualized' version of the old-style visions of the good society, a society hospitable to the humanity of its members. Hunting is a full-time task, it consumes a lot of attention and energy, it leaves little or no time for anything else; and so it averts attention from the unendingness of the task and postpones *ad calendas graecas* the moment of reflection during which the impossibility of the task ever being fulfilled would need to be faced point blank. As Blaise Pascal prophetically noted centuries ago, what people want is 'to be diverted from thinking of what they are . . . by some novel and agreeable passion which keeps them busy, like gambling, hunting, some absorbing show . . .' People want to escape the need to think of 'our unhappy condition', and so 'we prefer the hunt to the capture'. 'The hare itself will not save us from thinking' about the formidable but intractable faults in our shared condition, 'but hunting it does so'.

The snag is, though, that once tried, the hunt turns into a compulsion, an addiction and obsession. Catching a hare would be an anticlimax; it would only make the prospect of another hunt more seductive, since the hopes that accompany the hunt have been found to be the most delightful (the only delightful?) experience of the whole affair. Catching the hare presages an end to those hopes – unless another hunt is planned for the next day and started the next morning.

Is that the end of utopia? In one respect it is, in so far as the early modern utopias envisaged a point at which time would come to a stop; indeed, an end of time as *history*. There is no such point, though, in a hunter's life, no moment where one could say that the job had been completed, that the case was open and shut, the mission accomplished – and so could look forward to the rest of life as 'living happily ever after, from now to eternity'.

In addition, the prospect of an end to hunting is not tempting but frightening in a society of hunters – since such an end may arrive only in the form of a personal defeat and exclusion. The horns will go on announcing the start of another adventure, the greyhounds' bark will go on resurrecting the sweet memory of past chases, other people will go on hunting, there will be no end to the universal excitement . . . I'm the only one who will be stood aside, excluded and no longer wanted, barred from other people's joys: just a passive spectator on the other side of the fence, watching the party but forbidden or unable to join the revellers, enjoying the sights and sounds at best from a distance and by proxy.

If a life of continuing and continuous hunting is another utopia, it is – contrary to the utopias of the past – a utopia without an *end*. A bizarre utopia indeed, measured by orthodox standards; the original utopias derived their magnetic powers from their promise of an end to toil; the hunters' utopia is a dream of toil never ending.

A strange, unorthodox utopia – but a utopia all the same, promising the same unattainable prize brandished by all utopias, namely an ultimate and radical solution to human problems past, present and future, and an ultimate and radical cure for the sorrows and pains of the human condition. It is unorthodox mainly for having moved the land of solutions and cures from the 'faraway' into the 'here and now'. Instead of living *towards* a utopia, hunters are offered a living *inside* a utopia.

For the gardeners, utopia was the end of the road; for the hunters it is the road itself. Gardeners visualized the end of the road as the vindication and the ultimate triumph of utopia. For the hunters, the end of the road can only be the lived utopia's final, ignominious *defeat*. Adding insult to injury, it would also be a thoroughly *personal* defeat and clinching proof of personal failure. There is little if any prospect of other hunters stopping their hunting, and so the non-participation in the ongoing hunt can only feel like the ignominy of personal exclusion, and so (presumably) of personal inadequacy.

A utopia brought from the misty 'faraway' into the tangible 'here and now', a utopia *lived* rather than being *lived towards*, is immune to tests; for all practical intents and purposes, it is immortal. But its immortality has been achieved at the price of the frailty and vulnerability of each and all of those enchanted and seduced to live it.

Unlike the utopias of yore, the hunters' utopia does not offer a meaning to life, whether genuine or fraudulent. It only helps to chase the questions about life's meaning out of the minds of living. Having reshaped the course of life into an unending series of self-focused pursuits, each episode lived through as an overture to the next, it offers no occasion for reflection about the direction and sense of it all. When (if) such an occasion finally comes, at the moment of falling out of the hunting life, or being banned from it, it is usually too late for that reflection to bear on the way life – one's own as much as that of others – is shaped, and so too late to oppose its present shape and effectively dispute its propriety.

It is difficult, nay impossible, to sum up midway this unscripted and unfinished play with its still unravelling plot – a play in which we all are intermittently or simultaneously the accessories, the stage props, and the acting characters. But no one could claim to record better the dilemmas the players face than has already been done in the words given to Marco Polo by the great Italo Calvino in *La città invisibili*:

> The inferno of the living is not something that *will* be: if there is one, it is what is already here, the inferno where we live every day, that we form by being together. There are two ways to escape suffering it. The first is easy for many: accept the inferno and become such a part of it that you can no longer see it. The second is risky and demands constant vigilance and apprehension: seek and learn to recognize who and what, in the midst of the inferno, are not inferno, then make them endure, give them space.

> L'inferno dei viventi non è qualcosa che sarà; se ce n'è uno è quello que è già qui, l'inferno che abitiamo tutti i giorni, che formiamo stando insieme. Due modi ci sono per non soffrirne. Il primo riesce facile a molti: accettare l'inferno e diventarne parte fino al punto di non vederlo più. Il secondo è rischioso ed esige attenzione e apprendimento continui: cercare e saper riconoscere chi e cosa, in mezzo all'inferno, non è inferno, e farlo durare, e dargli spazio.

Whether living in a society of hunters does or does not feel like living in hell is of course a contentious matter; most seasoned hunters will tell you that being a hunter among hunters has its blissful moments . . . What is hardly a matter of contention, however, is that 'many' will go for the strategy 'easy for many', and so become 'part of it', no longer puzzled by its bizarre logic or irritated by its ubiquitous, obtrusive and in most cases fanciful demands. Also beyond doubt is the prospect that men and women who struggle to find out 'who and what are not hell' will need to face up to all sorts of pressures pushing them to accept what they insist on calling 'an inferno'.

Notes

1 Liquid Modern Life and its Fears

1 Milan Kundera, *L'Art du roman*, Gallimard, 1986.
2 Jacques Attali, *La Voie humaine*, Fayard, 2004.
3 Arundhati Roy, 'L'Empire n'est pas invulnérable', *Manière de Voir*, 75 (June–July 2004), pp. 63–6.
4 Quoted from Matthew J. Morgan, 'The garrison state revisited: civil–military implications of terrorism and security', *Contemporary Politics*, 10/1 (Mar. 2004), pp. 5–19.
5 See Alexander Hamilton, 'The consequences of hostilities between states', in *The Federalist Papers*, New American Library, 2003.
6 David L. Altheide, 'Mass media, crime, and the discourse of fear', *Hedgehog Review*, 5/3 (Fall 2003), pp. 9–25.
7 *Hedgehog Review*, 5/3 (Fall 2003), pp. 5–7.
8 Stephen Graham, 'Postmortem city: towards an urban geopolitics', *City*, 2 (2004), pp. 165–96.
9 Ray Surette, *Media, Crime and Criminal Justice*, Brooks/Cole, 1992, p. 43.
10 See Andy Beckett, 'The making of the terror myth', *Guardian*, G2, 15 Oct. 2004, pp. 2–3.
11 See Hugues Lagrange, *Demandes de sécurité*, Seuil, 2003.
12 See Victor Grotowicz, *Terrorism in Western Europe: In the Name of the Nation and the Good Cause*, PWN, Warsaw, 2000.
13 Michael Meacher, 'Playing Bin Laden's game', *Guardian*, 11 May 2004, p. 21.

14 See Maurice Druon, 'Les Stratégies aveugles', *Le Figaro*, 18 Nov. 2004, p. 13.

15 See Deborah Orr, 'A relentless diet of false alarms and terror hype', *Independent*, 3 Feb. 2004, p. 33.

16 See Duncan Campbell, 'The ricin ring that never was', *Guardian*, 14 Apr. 2005.

17 See 'War on terror fuels small arms trade', *Guardian*, 10 Oct. 2003, p. 19.

18 See Conor Gearty, 'Cry freedom', *Guardian*, G2, 3 Dec. 2004, p. 9.

19 See Benjamin R. Barber in conversation with Artur Domoslawski, *Gazeta Wyborcza*, 24–6 Dec. 2004, pp. 19–20.

2 Humanity on the Move

1 Rosa Luxemburg, *The Accumulation of Capital*, trans. Agnes Schwarzschild, Routledge, 1961, pp. 387, 416.

2 See Jeremy Seabrook, 'Powder keg in the slums', *Guardian*, 1 Sept. 2004, p. 10 (a fragment of the forthcoming book *Consuming Culture: Globalization and Local Lives*).

3 See Clifford Geertz, 'The use of diversity', in *Available Light: Anthropological Reflections on Philosophical Topics*, Princeton University Press, 2000, pp. 68–88.

4 At the time of the Gulf War, 'when Saddam turned his helicopter gunships on the Iraqi Kurds, they tried to flee north over the mountains into Turkey – but the Turks refused to let them in. They physically whipped them back at the border crossings. I heard one Turkish officer say, "We hate these people. They're fucking pigs." So for weeks the Kurds were stuck in the mountains at 10 below zero, often with only the clothes they were wearing when they fled. The children suffered the most: dysentery, typhoid, malnutrition . . .'(see Maggie O'Kane, 'The most pitiful sights I have ever seen', *Guardian*, 14 Feb. 2003, pp. 6–11).

5 Garry Younge, 'A world full of strangers', *Soundings* (Winter 2001–2), pp. 18–22.

6 See Alan Travis, 'Treatment of asylum seekers "is inhumane"', *Guardian*, 11 Feb. 2003, p. 7.

7 See Alan Travis, 'Blunkett to fight asylum ruling', *Guardian*, 20 Feb. 2003, p. 2.

8 See Michel Agier, *Aux bords du monde, les réfugiés*, Flammarion, 2002, pp. 55–6.

9 Ibid., p. 86.

10 See Fabienne Rose Émilie Le Houerou, 'Camps de la soif au Soudan', *Le Monde Diplomatique*, May 2003, p. 28.

11 Ibid., p. 94.

12 Ibid., p. 117.

13 Ibid., p. 120.

14 See Alan Travis, 'UK plan for asylum crackdown', *Guardian*, 13 June 2002.

15 Martin Bright, 'Refugees find no welcome in city of hate'. *Guardian*, 29 June 2003, p. 14.

16 See Alan Travis, 'Tough asylum policy "hits genuine refugees"', *Guardian*, 29 Aug. 2003, p. 11.

17 Gary Younge, 'Villagers and the damned', *Guardian*, 24 June 2002.

18 See Michel Foucault, 'Of other spaces', *Diacritics*, 1 (1986), p. 26.

19 See Loïc Wacquant, 'Symbole fatale. Quand ghetto et prison se ressemblent et s'assemblent', *Actes de la Recherche en Sciences Sociales* (Sept. 2001), p. 43.

20 Cf. Loïc Wacquant, 'The new urban color line: the state and fate of the ghetto in postfordist America', in Craig J. Calhoun (ed.), *Social Theory and the Politics of Identity*, Blackwell, 1994; also 'Elias in the dark ghetto', *Amsterdams Sociologisch Tidjschrift* (Dec. 1997).

21 See Michel Agier's 'Entre guerre et ville', *Ethnography*, 2 (2004).

22 Stewart Hall, 'Out of a clear blue sky', *Soundings* (Winter 2001–2), pp. 9–15.

23 David Garland, *The Culture of Control: Crime and Social Order in Contemporary Society*, Oxford University Press, 2001, p. 175.

24 Loïc Wacquant, 'Comment la "tolérance zéro" vint à l'Europe', *Manière de Voir* (Mar.–Apr. 2001), pp. 38–46.

25 Ulf Hedetoft, *The Global Turn: National Encounters with the World*, Aalborg University Press, 2003, pp. 151–2.

26 See Peter Andreas and Timothy Snyder, *The Wall around the West*, Rowman and Littlefield, 2000.
27 Naomi Klein, 'Fortress continents', *Guardian*, 16 Jan. 2003, p. 23. The article was first published in the *Nation*.

3 State, Democracy and the Management of Fears

1 Robert Castel, *L'Insécurité sociale. Qu'est-ce qu'être protégé?* Seuil, 2003, p. 5.
2 Sigmund Freud, *Civilization and its Discontents*, Penguin Freud Library, vol. 12, pp. 274ff.
3 Castel, *L'Insécurité sociale*, p. 6.
4 Ibid., p. 22.
5 For a fuller discussion, see my *Individualized Society*, Polity, 2002.
6 Ibid., p. 46.
7 See T. H. Marshall, *Citizenship and Social Class, and Other Essays*, Cambridge University Press, 1950.
8 Paolo Flores d'Arcais, 'The US elections: a lesson in political philosophy: populist drift, secular ethics, democratic politics' (here quoted from an MS translation by Giacomo Donis).
9 Cf. John Gledhill, 'Rights and the poor', in *Human Rights in Global Perspective: Anthropological Studies of Rights, Claims and Entitlement*, ed. Richard Ashby Wilson and Jon P. Mitchell, Routledge, 2003, pp. 210ff. (quoting C. B. Macpherson, *The Political Theory of Possessive Individualism: Hobbes to Locke*, Oxford University Press, 1962).
10 John R. Searle, 'Social ontology and free speech', *Hedgehog Review* (Fall 2004), pp. 55–66.
11 See Castel, *L'Insécurité sociale*, pp. 47ff.

4 Out of Touch Together

1 Nan Ellin, 'Fear and city building', *Hedgehog Review*, 5/3 (Fall 2003), pp. 43–61.
2 B. Diken and C. Laustsen, 'Zones of indistinction: security, terror and bare life', *Space and Culture*, 5 (2002), pp. 290–307.

3 G. Gumpert and S. Drucker, 'The mediated home in a global village', *Communication Research*, 4 (1996), pp. 422–38.

4 Stephen Graham and Simon Marvin, *Splintering Urbanism*, Routledge, 2001, p. 285.

5 Ibid., p. 15.

6 M. Schwarzer, 'The ghost wards: the flight of capital from history', *Thresholds*, 16 (1998), pp. 10–19.

7 Manuel Castells, *The Informational City*, Blackwell, 1989, p. 228.

8 Teresa Caldeira, 'Fortified enclaves: the new urban segregation', *Public Culture*, 8/2 (1996), pp. 303–28.

9 Nan Ellin, 'Shelter from the storm, or form follows fear and vice versa', in *Architecture of Fear*, ed. Nan Ellin, Princeton Architectural Press, 1997, pp. 13, 26.

10 Steven Flusty, 'Building paranoia', in *Architecture of Fear*, pp. 48–52.

11 See John Friedman, 'Where we stand: a decade of world city research', in *World Cities in a World System*, ed. P. L. Knox and P. J. Taylor, Cambridge University Press, 1995; David Harvey, 'From space to place and back again: reflections on the condition of postmodernity', in *Mapping the Futures*, ed. Jon Bird et al., Routledge, 1993.

12 Michael Peter Smith, *Transnational Urbanism: Locating Globalization*, Blackwell, 2001, pp. 54–5.

13 Ibid., p. 108.

14 Manuel Castells, *The Power of Identity*, Blackwell, 1997, pp. 61, 25.

15 Manuel Castells, 'Grassrooting the space of flows', in *Cities in the Telecommunications Age: The Fracturing of Geographies*, ed. J. O. Wheeler, Y. Aoyama and B. Warf, Routledge, 2000, pp. 20–1.

16 Richard Sennett, *The Uses of Disorder: Personal Identity and City Life*, Faber, 1996, pp. 39, 42.

17 Ibid., p. 194.

18 See Samuel Huntington, *The Clash of Civilizations and the Remaking of World Order*, Simon and Schuster, 1996.

19 See Mark Juergensmeyer, 'Is religion the problem?', *Hedgehog Review* (Spring 2004), pp. 21–33.